D1611624

A STUDY OF NAIMA

NEW YORK UNIVERSITY
STUDIES IN NEAR EASTERN CIVILIZATION
NUMBER 4

ALSO IN THIS SERIES

NUMBER I: F. E. Peters, Aristotle and the Arabs

NUMBER II: Jacob M. Landau, Jews in Nineteenth-Century Egypt

NUMBER III: Lois Anita Giffen, Theory of Profane Love Among the Arabs: The Development of the Genre

A Study of Naima

by

Lewis V. Thomas

Edited by

Norman Itzkowitz

NEW YORK UNIVERSITY PRESS

NEW YORK 1972

FOR ETHEL AND GLENN

Library of Congress Catalog Card Number: 71–189129

ISBN: 8147–8150–0

Manufactured in the United States of America

NEW YORK UNIVERSITY STUDIES IN NEAR EASTERN CIVILIZATION

The participation of the New York University Press in the University's new commitment to Near Eastern Studies—building on a tradition of well over a century—will provide Americans and others with new opportunities for understanding the Near East. Concerned with those various peoples of the Near East who, throughout the centuries, have dramatically shaped many of mankind's most fundamental concepts and who have always had high importance in practical affairs, this series, New York University Studies in Near Eastern Civilization, seeks to publish important works in this vital area. The purview will be broad, open to varied approaches and historical periods. It will, however, be particularly receptive to work in two aspects of near Eastern civilization that may have received insufficient attention elsewhere but which do reflect particular interests at New York University. These are literature and art. Furthermore, taking a stand that may be more utilitarian than that of other publications, the series will welcome both translations of important Near Eastern literature of imagination, and of significant scholarly works written in Near Eastern languages. In this way, a larger audience, unacquainted with these languages, will be able to deepen its knowledge of the cultural achievements of Near Eastern peoples.

R. Bayly Winder
Richard Ettinghausen
General Editors

Editor's Preface

Why see through to publication a doctoral thesis completed almost twenty-five years ago? That is a legitimate question, and the reply to it comes under several heads: the nature of the work itself, the position of Lewis V. Thomas in Ottoman studies in America, and my own relationship with him as my mentor.

His study of Naima was, when written, and is now a brilliant piece of scholarship. It is still the best thing available on Naima and on Ottoman historiography of the seventeenth and eighteenth centuries. Embodied in its pages are a view of Ottoman intellectual activity and self-awareness that has been neither equaled nor surpassed in the intervening almost quarter of a century. This may be a reflection on the state of Ottoman studies in general, but it is also an indication of the quality of Lewis V. Thomas' mind—his talent, insight, and perspicacity. The magnitude of Thomas' accomplishment is enhanced when we keep in mind the fact that he completed this study under the direction of the eminent Ottomanist Paul Wittek, at Brussels University in Belgium, during the first years of the aftermath of World War II with all that that implies. Why the author did not publish this study himself remains a mystery only partially explained by Thomas' known insistence upon perfection, especially perfection from himself, and the fact that he was his own severest critic. This work then stands on its own merits as a first-rate contribution to our knowledge of the Ottomans, and it has given me great pleasure to be able to present it to my colleagues in this field, especially to a new generation that did not have the opportunity to know its author personally.

I have sought to let Thomas speak for himself, intruding as editor only to render Turkish terms and names into modern Turkish, reduce the copious notation to manageable proportions, and to add some items of bibliography where it seemed appropriate.

Under the second heading it is important to note that Lewis V. Thomas' seminars in Ottoman studies at Princeton University were the main training ground for Ottomanists in America from 1950 until his death in 1965. After reading *A Study of Naima* one readily realizes the intellectual debt his students owe him, for in many instances their initial work is the amplification of ideas or notions set down in this work, or, if not here, then first generated in his seminars. I include myself in that student group. Thomas' was an imaginative, original, and fertile mind. He was never dogmatic, never insisted upon the primacy of his own view. Personally, I have disagreed in another place with his emphasis on the period 1683–99 as a crucial turning point in Ottoman history. Starting from the same point, Naima's introduction, I prefer to see 1774 and the defeat by the Russians in that light but his inspiration is obvious. Other students of his have also acknowledged their debt through the dedication of their work to his memory, and through us his influence will continue to permeate the field.

As a first-year graduate student at Princeton in 1953, I drifted into Lewis V. Thomas' orbit. The attraction of his mind and his superior intellect made me change my direction and embark upon a career in the Ottoman field. I have never had any misgivings, and my only regret is that his untimely death shortened our relationship. He asked me to act as his literary executor and edit whatever I considered publishable among his papers. The first publication that resulted was his *Elementary Turkish* (Cambridge, 1967), and now this study of Naima. I must thank R. Bayly Winder of New York University for his encouragement in my task. I have never wavered in my commitment to my mentor to publish his work. Rather, I have considered it the accomplishment of a *mitzva.*

NORMAN ITZKOWITZ

Princeton, New Jersey

Table of Contents

Abbreviations

EI	*Encyclopaedia of Islam*. 4 vols. Leiden-London, 1913–36. *Supplement*. Leiden, 1938.
EI²	*Encyclopaedia of Islam*. New Edition. Leiden, 1960–.
GOR	J. von Hammer. *Geschichte des Osmanischen Reiches*. 10 vols. Pesth, 1827–35.
GOW	Franz Babinger. *Die Geschichtsschreiber des Osmanen und Ihre Werke*. Leipzig, 1927.
İA	*İslâm Ansiklopedisi*. Istanbul, 1941–.
Islam	*Der Islam*. Strassburg, etc., 1910–.
MOG	*Mitteilungen zur Osmanischen Geschichte*. 2 vols. Vienna-Hanover, 1921–5.
OTD	Mehmet Zeki Pakalın. *Osmanlı Tarih Deyimleri ve Terimleri Sözlüğü*. 3 vols. Istanbul, 1946.
SO	Mehmed Sürreya. *Sicill-i Osmanî*. 4 vols. Constantinople, 1308–15/1890–98.
TOEM	*Tarih-i Osmanî Encümeni Mecmuası*. 7 vols. Constantinople 1329– /1911–31.
TTV	*Türk Tarih Vesikaları*. 3 vols. Istanbul, 1941–58.

Introduction

1. Editions and Manuscripts

Mustafa Naima's chronicle of Ottoman history, one of the most popular Ottoman prose works, has been printed in full three times.[1] The later editions are based on the first and differ from it only in details. Special note should be made of the revised (nineteenth-century) spelling of the third edition. The third edition is the most easily procurable and by far the most legible of the three.[2] References in this study are to that edition except where otherwise noted. The first edition was from the pioneer Ottoman press (İbrahim Müteferrika) and was printed less than twenty years after Naima's death. It was the thirteenth Ottoman work and the fourth historical work printed in Turkey.[3] Manuscripts of Naima are relatively numerous; some of them prove to be transcribed from the first printed edition.[4]

2. Naima's Reputation and Popularity

Muslim history, especially Ottoman history, was traditionally one of the most popular branches of literature among the Ottomans as it is among the Turks today. Naima seems always to have been read. For example, Penah Efendi (Süleyman ibn Mustafa), whose proposals for the restoration of the state are among the most interesting of later eighteenth-century Ottoman records,[5] had not only read Naima[6] but derives his view of history directly from the ideas summarized in Naima's two prefaces.

As a favorite work of Ottoman prose, Naima's history maintained its prestige even where direct Ottoman rule was no longer popular. In 1256/1840–1 in Cairo certain officials of the khedive's personal staff proved to be inadequately trained. They were sent back to school. Among their required assignments was a daily stint of ten to twenty minutes' reading in Naima.[7]

Naima continued to be read and admired in the late nineteenth century. Ebüzziya, speaking of the historian Ahmet Cevdet Pasha, contends that of the some 600 historians who had lived during the preceding six centuries, none might be compared to Cevdet Pasha except those "of the very first rank, including Naima."[8] In the same way, the later Ottoman encyclopaedist Şemseddin Sami calls Naima "the loftiest of Ottoman historians."[9]

Although Naima has been published recently in the new Turkish alphabet, doubtlessly the text is partially unintelligible to the average Turkish reader despite the relative simplicity of Naima compared with most Ottoman prose. Hence it cannot truthfully be said that Naima is still popular today. He belongs to a literature which in another generation will probably be entirely dead. But his name is nonetheless still esteemed.

M. Fuad Köprülü, the leading modern Turkish student of the Ottomans, singled out Naima as the one Ottoman historian "who possessed descriptive powers of the first order" and who "gives vivid historical analyses of historical characters."[10] This view is taught in Turkey's schools. For example, in the standard upper-school text of Gönensay and Banarlı, the authors reproduce Professor Köprülü's opinion and add: "Although Naima wrote his work as official historian, he did not hesitate to portray events as they really took place, but showed that he had the courage to depict the real nature of even the most degenerate and ugly happenings."[11]

Naima is one of the few Ottoman writers known even by name beyond the limits of the Ottoman Empire. A part of his history has been published in an English translation and extracts have appeared in other western languages.[12] The English translation unfortunately is completely unreliable; no use has been made of it in this study.[13]

Perhaps the most interesting recent judgment on Naima is that of the Turkish novelist and teacher Halide Edip (Mrs. A. Adnan Adıvar). In her *Memoirs* (p. 232), she speaks of ". . . Naima, the wonderful Turkish chronicler who reaches to the levels of Shakesperian psychological penetration in his simple yet vivid description . . . , his almost incomprehensible and very formless old prose. . . . [When] I could penetrate the hard crust of his language, and . . . his critical and intensely living presentation of facts emerged . . . , [it became] a wonderful vision of individual souls, larger crowds, and revolutions in life and action." And (p. 262) "Naima shows in one single revolutionary scene a singular power of representing the setting as well as the thoughts and the feelings of his time with an understanding which would sound true and real in any age, although the Turkish press of the period in its loose and primitive form of the day was hardly a fit instrument to express such a perfect picture of real life."

İbrahim Müteferrika, Naima's first publisher, himself informs us that Naima's history was popular among the Ottomans almost from the start. Its general popularity, its intrinsic merit, and the fact that manuscripts were scarce and expensive were what led Müteferrika to print it rather than "other histories."[14]

3. The Present Study

The following study includes an account of Naima's life, an analysis of his two prefaces and of the structure of his chronicle, a statement on Naima's thought, information on his sources, and an attempt to evaluate his accomplishment.

NOTES

1. *Ravzat el-Hüseyin fi hulâsât ahbâr el-hâfikayn,* commonly called *Tarih-i Naima.* First ed.: Müteferrika Press, 2 vols., f° Constantinople, 1147/1733. Second and third eds.: Amire Press, 6 vols., 8°, Constantinople, 1280/1863–4. and 1281–3/1864–6 respectively. In addition, the first volume of the Müteferrika edition was reprinted at Constantinople in 1259/1843. See *GOW,* 246; J. Rypka, *Bakí als Ghazeldichter,* p. 189, n. 1. Published in New Letters, *Naima Tarihi,* Zuhuri Danışman, ed., 6 vols.

2. Noted by M. Belin, "Bibliographie Ottomane," *Journal Asiatique,* 6. Ser. XI (June, 1868), 486.

3. See F. Meninski, *Lexicon arabico-persico-turcicum,* B. Jenisch, ed. I, lxxxvii, n. y; and Selim Nüzhet Gerçek, *Türk Matbaacılığı,* pp. 84–5.

4. For manuscripts reported in European collections, see *GOW,* 246. Twenty-one Istanbul manuscripts are described in Türkiye Cumhuriyeti, Maarif Vekilliği Kütüphaneler Müdürlüğü Tasnif Komisyonu, *Istanbul Kütüphaneleri Tarih-Coğrafya Yazmaları Katalogları,* "Turkce Tarih Yazmaları," 200 *seq.* See also M. Münir Aktepe, "Naimâ Tarihi'nin yazma nushaları hakkında," *Tarih Dergisi,* I/1 (1949), 35–52.

5. Edited and annotated by Aziz Berker under the title "Mora Ihtilâli Tarihçesi," *TTV*, II/8 (1942–3), 63–80, 153–60, 228–40, 309–20, 385–400, 473–80. The work includes an eye-witness account of the Russian landing in the Morea in 1770.

6. Penah Efendi, *TTV*, II/8 (1942), 159.

7. A Cairo *defter* of 1256/began March 5, 1840, quoted in J. Deny, *Sommaire des Archives Turques du Caire*, p. 97.

8. Quoted from Ebülûlâ Mardin, *Ahmet Cevdet Paşa*, p. 24, n. 43.

9. Şemseddin Sami, *Kamus el-Âlem*, VI, 4593–4.

10. *EI*, IV, 952.

11. Hıfzı Tevfik Gönensay and Nihad Sami Banarlı, *Türk Edebiyatı Tarihi* (*Başlangıçtan Tanzimata Kadar*), p. 156/ . See Section 25, below.

12. Mustafa Naima, *Annals of the Turkish Empire from 1591–1659 of the Christian Era*, Charles Fraser, trans. (London, 1832). See *GOW*, 246, for information on extracts published in Russian, Hungarian, and Swedish, and on a complete translation (in manuscript) in French.

13. Compare the review by J. von Hammer, quoted in Johann Wilhelm Zinkeisen, *Geschichte des Osmanischen Reiches in Europa,* III, 663, n. 1.

14. Müteferrika's preface, Naima, I, 15 (separately paged). Professor Philip Hitti informs me that later Arab historians not infrequently used Naima. It is certain that he was widely read.

CHAPTER ONE
Life

4. Introduction

Mustafa Naima was born about 1665 in Aleppo, son of the janissary commander of that place. As a young man he went to Istanbul and entered the Palace service, obtaining the advantageous post of an apprentice secretary in the halberdier corps. He was early interested in Ottoman history. That interest eventually brought him the patronage of two grand vezirs, Hüseyin Köprülü and Moralı Hasan, and it was to them that Naima dedicated the two volumes of his history. Moralı Hasan's dismissal from the grand vezirate (1704) appears virtually to have terminated Naima's work as a professional historian. Thereafter he had a sporadically successful career as an Ottoman civil administrator until his death (1716) at about the age of fifty.[1]

5. Naima's Grandfather

Naima's grandfather, Küçük Ali Agha, a prosperous janissary officer of Aleppo, and Naima's father, Mehmed Agha, janissary commander of Aleppo, are known only through references in Naima's history.[2] The grandfather appears in a section dealing with the year 1644 (Section 6, below). This passage shows unusually close knowledge of Aleppo life and takes special pains to explain details that would not readily be understood by the ordinary Ottoman reader. Without hesitation it may be regarded as almost entirely Naima's own composition, one of the longest original sections in the whole of his compiled chronicle.

6. **Emir Assaf**

From Naima, IV, 104–10. Year 1054 (began March 10, 1644)

The Affair of the Desert Chief Assaf at Aleppo

The padishah, Asylum of the Universe, when he proceeded to the pleasure grounds at Edirne, bestowed the province of Aleppo and the rank of vezir upon İbrahim Pasha the privy-armsbearer.[3] *İbrahim Pasha thereupon went to Aleppo where he undertook to assure himself full control of the government of the province. At that time an outstanding figure was the Emir Assaf,*[4] *chief of the nomad Arabs who dwelt in the region around Aleppo.*[5] *Assaf avoided the lands where one found vezirs and emirs, but he mercilessly taxed the villages of Arabistan, claiming both taxes*[6] *and "brotherhood."*[7] *In addition to this, during the period of Emir Assaf's control there had been no lack of tyranny and excess on the part of Arab brigands and no want of highway robbery and mischief. In short, Emir Assaf was a man whom it would be difficult to dislodge.*

The governor of Aleppo, İbrahim Pasha, realized that Assaf would neither accept deposition nor yet come under the sword of policy. Of his own ready inspiration, İbrahim Pasha had recourse to a dishonorable measure. He thenceforth gave Assaf many assurances, speaking to him as if from a pure heart, and he sent to him a man to invite him to a feast.[8]

Assaf, on his part, had not been sure of the governor prior to this. And now, since negotiations in this matter were not in the hands of some recognized leading citizen of Aleppo upon whose word he could rely, he became alarmed. He sent word to the pasha, saying, "We are Arabs of the sort accustomed to the desert and the open lands. We have never ventured into the great lands or close to cities. May his honor the pasha excuse us from coming to the feast. For us, the prospect of going into Aleppo is frightening." Assaf also sent the pasha several horses, and so excused himself.

The pasha then called in a dignitary of Aleppo, a man named Deli Kurd,[9] *and said to him, "Go out and bring that Arab to terms. And when you have got him to trust in our assurances, bring him in for our feast."*

Deli Kurd answered, "My sultan,[10] *the Arabs don't come in close to Aleppo. If I am even able to get him to come to a place no farther than a day's journey away from Aleppo, it will mean that he has believed my word."*

The pasha replied, "Go on, now. Let the feast be held at any place to which you can get him to come." And so he sent him off.

Deli Kurd made his way to Assaf. Whatever it was that Deli Kurd told Assaf, the latter came to a decision and promised to come to a place called . . . ,[11] *some five hours out from Aleppo.*

The pasha, on his part, sent to that place many tents and cooks and all else that was needed for the feast, several days in advance. The people of the whole city also set out with great preparations, saying, "The pasha is giving a feast to the padishah of the desert." Hence, the people dressed in their best, mounted caparisoned horses, and started out for the site of the feast—wave after wave of them, as if they were going for an outing in the countryside.

On the day set, the pasha also mounted his horse and left the city with a great procession, all the levends, iç-oğlans, *and city-aghas.*[12]

Earlier, at sunrise, Deli Kurd had come to the pasha and said, "My sultan, if it is your intention to kill Assaf, that is out of the question at this time, for you have given him a written safe-conduct as well as the towel[13] *and he—after the ancient custom of the Arabs—has put the written safe-conduct in his bosom and the towel around his neck in token that he comes as one who is henceforth under your protection. The Arab folk are no longer mere ignorant fellows as they used to be. Most of them know everything about deceitful stratagems. It is likely that Assaf will come with a large number of Arabs attending him. Should it appear that you, on your part, are going to make any attempt on him, it will be difficult for you to get the upper hand. If we do have to fight, our soldiers are not ready. What I fear is that there may be a disaster. The wise course is that, for this time, the ritual of formal conversation and of the exchange of gifts should be carried through and then, at some time hereafter, Assaf should be dealt with by other means. Apart from this, if it should come to be said of you that the pasha is a man who does not keep his word or honor the safe-conduct which he himself has issued, you will henceforth be unable to control or subdue the tribes of any region." So Deli Kurd spoke at length.*

But the pasha was a real "Your Excellency" and of a decidedly stubborn nature.[14] *He reprimanded Deli Kurd, saying, "You may be sure that when we kill a man whom we have invited to a feast, that is the right thing to do!" and so he silenced him.*

Deli Kurd replied, "You know best," and went out.

Everyone then proceeded to the battleground, that is to the place of the feast. Now the pasha commanded his guard—water-carriers[15] *and musketeers—to load with double-shot the parade arms which they bore.*

When Assaf would have to come to kiss the stirrup and would then turn away, four of the guard were to shoot him down, firing simultaneously. And they did so load their arms and were ready and prepared.

As the pasha and his retinue drew near from the one side, Assaf Bey came up from the other, accompanied in his turn by more than six thousand lance-bearing, black-garbed Arab horsemen. The treasure of the Arab chieftains is a number of suits of mail armor. It is their custom always to carry these on camels by the side of whoever is the chief, when they migrate. They also have a large desert-tent woven of black hair. This serves them as a hall in which the divan may meet. This tent and those suits of armor are the chief's emblems of authority.

Assaf had had his Arabs don these suits of mail and several thousands of them were armed to the teeth with swords and the like.

When the pasha and his retinue approached the feast-tent, Assaf Bey and several hundred of his mail-clad Arabs separated themselves from the other Arabs, who stayed at the far end of the field. Assaf himself spurred his horse forward, dismounting when he came into the pasha's presence. He then walked forward so that he might take hold of the pasha's stirrup. The pasha also made to dismount, and while they were moving towards the feast-tent, the water-carriers and musketeers who had loaded their firearms with double-shot made ready.

When Assaf came to kiss the pasha's skirt, two muskets were suddenly discharged into his breast and a third, from behind, into his flank. Now this Arab was a devilishly tall man—like a minaret—and so he was not knocked down by the impact of these shots, since under his clothes he also had put on three of these shirts of mail. The shots had penetrated one shirt but had been caught in the others and so had had no effect within [*i.e., had not wounded Assaf*]. *At once the Arab realized what he had to deal with. He drew his sword; the Arabs who were with him formed a circle around him and got him as far as his horse. He mounted and then, with his men, bore down upon the group of men beside the pasha. After these Arabs had killed more than twenty of the* iç-ağas *and the pasha's men, they made off towards the other Arabs who were lined up at the protected end of the plain.*

To them Assaf cried, "Come on![16] *These scoundrels have wronged me!" And at once these many thousands of Arab cavaliers shouted out "The bastard!"*[17] *with a single voice and raised a frightful screech to the skies, brandishing their lances.*

The pasha was in the middle of his troop. The Arabs fell upon the many thousands of horsemen who were round about. Every man whose horse was swift made off for the Aleppo road, escaped, and was saved. The Arabs also sped down the Aleppo road, but some of them headed for the pasha's troop. Its soldiers resisted them and there was a fight. After several men had perished on each side, the Arabs withdrew and the pasha also got to Aleppo.

The feast-tents and the provisions, many things to eat already cooked, and the cooking utensils too, were all plundered by the Arabs. Most of the people who had gone out from Aleppo to see the Arabs lost their horses and their clothes. Many of them were cut to pieces and died.

Thus a great disaster did take place.

Thereafter Emir Assaf did not put his trust in non-Ottomans, but he did make it more and more plain that he was in revolt.[18] *Other Arabs also took courage and began to do more mischief and more wickedness than before.*

When news of this was rumored in the capital, they deposed İbrahim Pasha and transferred Aleppo province to Derviş Mehmed Pasha who had been removed from the governorship of Baghdad and was now sent to Aleppo.

My late father, the serdar *of Aleppo, Mehmed Agha, used to tell this story: "At the time of the Assaf affair, I was in the troop of İbrahim Pasha. Of the pasha's men only twenty or thirty were killed and some forty or fifty of those who were left behind were stripped. But most of the city men who had gone out for the show were stripped and many of them were wounded."*

Later on, the government turned a gracious face to Assaf. This attitude was assumed as a measure of policy. Still later, Bektaş Agha, the kethuda *bey, came forward as Assaf's protector and became his official representative in Istanbul.*[19] *When Assaf's firman of confirmation was granted, Bektaş Agha sent my grandfather, Küçük Ali Agha, to communicate the order of confirmation to Assaf Bey, picking my grandfather because he was an able, outstanding citizen of Aleppo. Bektaş Agha ordered him to use such measures as would bring Assaf back again into the circle of obedience.*

On that occasion my father accompanied my grandfather into the desert. When they reached Assaf, the emir—as was the custom—drew up his troops having clothed his Arabs in armor, and formally received the imperial firman and the robe of honor.

In the session of friendly conversation which followed Assaf's reception of the firman and the robe, my grandfather spoke plainly to him, saying, "To be counted as obedient to the sublime state is the fundamental pride of all the peoples of the state. Since the line of Abu Rish is the root and race of the Arabs and of the bedouins and of the tribes which keep their oaths, and since there lives not a single man who would consider that it befitted your band to step beyond the sphere of good conduct, whatever was *it that caused such matters of evil consequence to happen?"*[20]

When he had begun to give Assaf all sorts of advice and admonishment, Emir Assaf replied: "Ah! By Ali and by God, I am not to blame.[21] *İbrahim Pasha gave me his promise of a truce and invited me to a feast. God knows that I went to him intending to serve him from that day forward with complete loyalty." Then Assaf called out, "Bring in that armor," and they produced the three mail shirts he had worn on the day of the agreement.*

"I looked them over," related Küçük Ali Agha, "and one of those bullets which had hit the breastplate had pierced the first of the three coats of mail and lodged in the other two. Little nail-like slivers had been driven on in. On the back part of the armor Assaf showed us a similar bullet, saying, 'By the Lord of the Kaaba! Thanks to the impact of those bullets I vomited blood for two months. What wrong had I done, for him to betray me so?' Thus he complained about İbrahim Pasha."

Ali Agha consoled him, saying, "The masters of fortune know your worth.[22] *They would never assent to your execution. This was a bad business, but it's all done and finished with. From now on, the responsibility that is yours is to render obedient service and to keep the bedouins under your control." So Ali Agha cheered Assaf, adding, "It is certain that the Sublime State did not consent in İbrahim Pasha's evil attempt against you and it is plain that it was for your sake that he was removed from Aleppo province. Henceforth you should behave manfully so as to prove your words of allegiance." Thus with a thousand clever phrases he calmed the heart of the Arab and brought him over to the side of obedience and friendship.*

Not only did Assaf send many mares and horses to the capital as gifts, but he also gave to Ali Agha and to my father ten horses, six mares, and two thousand pieces of gold. He said, moreover, "May I pay the two thousand gold by written order on Aleppo? I haven't any cash by me." And he gave them a letter [to his banker in Aleppo]. Thus in addition to all the horses and mares and other gifts, he honored them with ten thousand kuruş *in cash.*

7. Ottoman Provincial Society

This narrative not only identifies Mustafa Naima's family, but also illustrates important features of the seventeenth-century Ottoman provincial environment in which he grew up.[23] His family was "in politics." Hence provincial politics particularly interest us here. One sees certain disadvantages under which an Ottoman governor had to work. Appointed for an indefinite but probably short term and paying heavily for his appointment, he had not only to reimburse himself quickly, but simultaneously to devote much energy and money to maintaining his own political fences in Istanbul. In this environment he did not have absolute authority.[24] Also where, as was the case at Aleppo, a large part of the population did not know Turkish, the ordinary governor had to rely upon paid translators or else work through members of the bilingual Ottoman community permanently resident in the province. These men could scarcely be expected to put the governor's interests ahead of their own unless the governor were prepared to make this worth their while. At the same time, many such men—as was the case with Naima's grandfather—had their direct connections with powerful Istanbul elements who might be working actively at the capital against the governor's interests.

Apart from all this, the governor had to deal with the provincial mentality of men who, although they were loyal Ottomans, still lived permanently on the spot and so were not only well informed as to local matters but also convinced that they knew what should be done and how to do it better than did any outsider.

At best, even in times of genuine prosperity and peace, the well-to-do Ottoman provincial society in which Naima spent his formative years was perilously complex. Hidden currents of personal ambition and intrigue which moved it truly made it a quicksand for the feet of all but the wisest and most provident. It was an ideal environment for the education of a future Ottoman historian.

In such a community Naima's family had obtained a position of standing and prosperity. They preserved this position for at least two generations and were able to procure for a scion of the third generation, Naima, one of the best opportunities that Istanbul then had to offer—a good apprentice post in the Palace service.

It is also clear that the family were loyal Ottomans, by which one means that they were Muslim Turkish servants of the Ottoman dynasty and state. They were bilingual, speaking Arabic and Ottoman Turkish. The grandfather and the father emerge as politician-janissaries rather than as fighting janissaries. Naima nowhere injects a personal word referring to any military exploits of his janissary family. The grandfather and father apparently had families and permanent homes. They exemplify many of the fundamental alterations in janissary life which began to become widespread immediately after, if not during, the reign of Süleyman the Magnificent (1520–66).[25]

8. **Naima's Father**

Naima gives us a further glimpse of his family in a passage (Section 9) describing an experience of his father's at janissary headquarters in Istanbul on the eve of Sultan İbrahim's dethronement (1648).[26] Mehmed Agha's presence in Istanbul at this time was possibly connected with the family's role in the relations between Emir Assaf and his Istanbul protector, Bektaş Agha. It may be that a result of this trip was the appointment of Mehmed Agha to be janissary commander in Aleppo. Certainly the narrative here is Naima's own composition, one of several additions made at this point by Naima and by his predecessor-compiler, Şarih al-Manarzade, to the original source's account of how Hezarpare Ahmed Pasha, grand vezir to the wastrel Sultan İbrahim, was attempting to compel various important dignitaries and officials to contribute to the treasury—money, ambergris, furs, and the like—luxuries which the extravagant sultan demanded but which the treasury was too empty to provide.

9. **The Ocak Aghas**

From Naima, IV, 295–6. Year 1058 (began January 27, 1648)

At this juncture the wise vezir exacted from Bektaş Agha, Musliheddin Agha, Murad Agha, and Kara Çavuş Agha—all of them ocak *aghas—a contribution of royal furs (sables, as stipulated) and also of purses.*[27] *The* ocak *aghas were angered at this severe action. They discussed these dis-*

couraging events among themselves and, having girded up the skirt of agreement, came to detest the vezir and to be ready to rouse the flames of revolt.

My father, the late Serdar Mehmed Agha, used to relate the following: "Kara Murad Agha, who had come from Crete, was a handsomely dressed man of great stature, the chief stay of the ocak *aghas and an awe-inspiring man. He headed a band of over five hundred personal adherents and he was an outstanding, impressive man whose words the janissaries generally heeded.*

"One day I was present in his circle when a messenger came from the defterdar.[28] *The messenger kissed Murad Agha's skirt and put into his hands a communication from the divan.*

"Murad Agha asked, 'What's this?'

"The messenger haughtily replied, 'They have sent for the two sable kapanices *and the ambergris and the cash contribution which are required of you, my honorable sultan, as state-aid,' adding, 'Please deliver them without delay.'*[29]

"Kara Murad Agha's eyes became blood-stones. He answered impetuously: 'Go and say to the defterdar efendi that I have come from Crete. All that I own is oily bullets and they are slick with a fine powder-gloss—nothing more! We in Crete hear the words "sables" and "ambergris" from the mainland, but we have never seen any. And if you speak of money . . . we receive that, as religion stipulates, and we spend it as we get it. Take our greetings to the defterdar efendi and say to him what I have said to you.'[30]

"While the messenger considered whether he should say something more to Karalı Murad, the agha roared, 'Get out!' with a shout that shook the room like an earthquake. All of us [added Naima's father] were changed and saddened, for it was evident that all the ocak *aghas had agreed to slip the bridle from the neck of obedience."*

10. **Janissary Aghas**

The janissary aghas of this passage represent power and wealth as great as the leaders of that corps ever attained. They epitomize the loyalties and standards of the corps whose tradition must have been alive in the family in which Naima grew up. The importance of the janissary aghas had been increasing throughout the period of the "Women's Sultanate," a period which may conveniently be taken as extending from the murder of Mehmed Sokollu (1579) to the beginning of Mehmed Köprülü's grand vezirate (1656), and thus including almost the entire span covered by Naima's history. During this three-quarters of a century ultimate power ordinarily rested in the hidden hands of a palace machine. It had now become the exception rather than the rule for the sultan himself to enter directly and actively into the administration of affairs for any prolonged period of time. His family and intimates—the sultan's women, servants, and courtiers—soon came really to control and exploit the state. Originally the important janissary aghas served as indispensable agents for the Palace machine. From agent to master was a short step. By the date of Naima's father's visit to Istanbul (1648), the aghas had almost succeeded in taking this step. Bektaş Agha provides an instructive case in point. He was outstanding in war, in political power, in greed, in personal wealth, and—eventually—in merited unpopularity.[31]

Like the other three aghas of the passage,[32] Bektaş Agha was a "regular" janissary in the sense that he was non-Muslim born and had been regularly trained in the janissary system. But he was married, and to the daughter of another important janissary agha.[33] This, strictly speaking, was irregular, but it was common. Naima gives no information regarding his own great-grandfather. This is probably an indication that Naima's grandfather, Küçük Ali Agha, like the great aghas of his time, was a "regular" janissary—a boy not born a Muslim, but who had come into the Ottoman state and the Muslim community as an apprentice trained through the janissary organization. Naima naturally preserves polite silence about his grandmother and his mother, but again it is not inadmissible to speculate that what was true of the great aghas at headquarters was also likely to be true of their subordinates at Aleppo and that the women in Naima's family may themselves have come from janissary families. In any event, this tendency among all sorts of Ottomans to marry into families that belonged to the same branch of state service—the same class—as their own families is too pronounced and too important to be dismissed without mention.

Bektaş Agha's death symbolizes the eventual failure of the janissary corps to win and wield ultimate power in the Ottoman state. It was the murder (1651) of Kösem Sultan—the "Old Queen Mother," mother of Murad IV and İbrahim, grandmother of Mehmed IV, herself for a generation and more the central figure and dominating personality of the Women's Sultanate and the chief protectress of the *ocak* aghas[34]—it was the murder of this striking woman that led to Bektaş Agha's destitution and execution. Others of the *ocak* aghas weathered that premonitory storm. Kara Murad was even to serve two short terms as grand vezir (1649–50 and 1655), before Mehmed Köprülü finally curbed the *ocak* aghas' political power.

11. Janissary Serdar

Naima's father apparently became janissary commander (*serdar*) for Aleppo while the great aghas with whom his family was connected were still at the height of their power. His new position was scarcely important on the imperial scale, but it was in the Aleppo world. It brought financial advantages and local prestige which were the immediate backdrop for Naima's boyhood and young manhood.[35]

A janissary *serdar* was the absolute commander of all the janissaries in his jurisdiction (the *kaza*). He was answerable only to the Istanbul headquarters and not to the provincial governor. Upon the *serdar* devolved not only the discipline and the mustering into service of all janissaries under his jurisdiction, but also the control of their estates, execution of their testaments, and protection of their often very considerable financial interests.[36] Hence the office of *serdar* in Aleppo is to be regarded as a valuable plum. The appointment, of course, was purchased, probably in much the same fashion stipulated in the later document which follows (dated 1231/1815–16):

From of old, the time-honored payments for the office of serdar *set in the various* kazas *have been assigned especially, to be fixed revenue, to the janissary headquarters of my Sublime Porte. Therefore it is established practice that* serdars *are not to be appointed by* buyuruldu [*"decree," such as a* vali *might issue*] *or by* mürasele [*"letter," such as a kadi might issue*], *but the appointment is to be notified to my imperial corps, the customary payment is to be sent, the letter of appointment to the position of* serdar *is to be obtained from the corps, and the usual payments are to be made thereafter once every three months, or every six months, or once yearly. . . .*[37]

12. To Istanbul

How long Ali Agha served at Aleppo and what the effect of the Köprülü regime was upon Naima's family are open questions. It was not until about 1685, when the administration of the first two—and greatest—Köprülüs, Mehmed (1656–61) and his son Fazil Ahmed (1661–76), had been followed by the disastrous failure of the Köprülü protégé Kara Mustafa at the siege of Vienna (1683), that young Mustafa Naima went from Aleppo to Istanbul to make his way in the life of the capital.

Naima's motive is not clear. Assuming that the family had preserved its fortune and political influence—and this seems probable since young Naima found easy entry into an advantageous and doubtless costly Palace post and into influential circles in Istanbul—one still wonders why he did not follow his grandfather and father in a janissary career. Was it ambition that led him to consider the janissary organization of his day a has-been, a career no longer as attractive as in the days of the Women's Sultanate? Was he attracted to Istanbul in response to growing centralization in the Ottoman system? Or was the principal factor the personal temperament of the future historian, a temperament naturally inclined toward the life of a "man of the pen" rather than that of a "man of the sword"?

Whatever his reasons, Naima now left Aleppo the Grey for Istanbul, the Abode of Felicity and the center of the breathtaking opportunities that the Ottoman Empire still had to offer an able young man.

13. Tayyarzade's Life

The best and fullest account of Naima's life is that preserved in the nineteenth-century *Tarih-i Atâ* by Tayyarzade who reproduces in full an otherwise unreported life of Naima by Şehrizade Mehmed Said.[38]

Sehrizade was the eighteenth-century historian who, according to Tayyarzade, reworked Naima's draft chronicle for the years 1070–1110/1660–1699. Thus at least part of the following account may ultimately rest on autobiographical passages found in that draft chronicle and perhaps in other writings of Naima.[39]

From *Tarih-i Atâ*, III, 36–8

Biography of the Historian Naima Efendi

According to the account in Şehrizade Said Efendi's little history called the Nevpeyda,[40] *the historian Naima Efendi set foot in the mortal world in the famous city of Aleppo the Grey.*[41] *He came to the Threshold of Felicity in the time of the fullness of his youth and about* 1100 [*began October* 26, 1688] *entered the body of the halberdiers of the Old Palace.*[42] *At the college in the imperial mosque of Sultan Bayezid*[43] *he worked perseveringly to complete his education and he attained distinction, thanks to his natural aptitude. Thereafter he went forth from the imperial palace*[44] *and was rewarded with the post of divan secretary to Kalaylıkoz Ahmed Pasha and with the rank of bureau chief.*[45] *Later, during the time when Rami Mehmed Pasha was chief secretary for foreign affairs,*[46] *Naima was frequently in the company of the said Rami Mehmed Pasha and of the kazasker for Rumeli Yahya Efendi.*[47] *Also, thanks to his skill in the science of the stars, Naima was associated with the dignitaries of the reign of Sultan Mustafa Han II. Thus Naima ascended to the vault of success.*

Through the exertions of the said Rami Mehmed Pasha, Naima obtained a daily stipend of 120 *full aspers from the Istanbul customs funds.*[48] *Amcazade Hüseyin Pasha, who became grand vezir in* 1109, *chose him for the post of official historian.*[49] *He composed and presented to Hüseyin Pasha the preface of the history which is known by his name. Upon its being accepted, there was bestowed upon Naima five hundred* kuruş *largess together with an imperial diploma ordering that another* kuruş *be added to his daily stipend from the customs funds.*[50] *Thus he attained the preface of prosperity.*

In 1116 [*began May* 6, 1704] *during the grand vezirate of Kalaylıkoz Ahmed Pasha, Damad İbrahim Pasha was secretary to the agha of the abode of felicity, Tavil Süleyman Agha; that is, İbrahim Pasha was secretary for the imperial pious foundations of the two Sacred Places.*[51] *In consequence of the friendship of İbrahim Pasha, who was originally from the halberdier corps, for Naima, İbrahim Pasha and the said Grand Vezir Kalaylıkoz Ahmed Pasha together took action and gladdened Naima by conferring upon him the post of chief of the Anadolu accountant's bureau, one of the divan posts.*[52]

Halberdier Mehmed Pasha, the grand vezir whose term of office followed the eighty-day grand vezirate of the said Ahmed Pasha, dismissed the said Naima and banished him to Gallipoli.[53] *This was because certain horoscopes which Naima, in connection with his practice of astrology, had drawn up had called forth the professional enmity of his colleagues.*[54] *But when he who among grand vezirs is worthy to be named "foremost of the foremost," Çorlulu Ali Pasha the martyr, the perspicacious, marked by dignities, heaven-dwelling, honored the station of the grand vezirate, he pardoned and released Naima and honored him with the post of master of ceremonies.*[55] *Moreover, since at that time the duty of the mastership of ceremonies was not important enough to be counted and regarded as one of the more important posts—as it is today—and since it did not carry a great income or a large stipend, Ali Pasha joined to it the post of keeper of records for the* kalyons[56] *so as to increase Naima's pay, and thus singled out Naima from among his colleagues.*

Naima thereafter came to be in favor with Silihdar Ali Pasha the martyr, the kindly, that Ali Pasha who had originally come from the barracks of the private cellar in the imperial Inner Palace and had risen from the post of confidential secretary to be armsbearer, imperial son-in-law, and, on the fourth of Rebiyülevvel 1125 [*April* 27, 1713], *to the station of the grand vezirate.*[57] *Naima had entered the wisdom-attracting,* Baykara-*pleasing circle of Ali Pasha, a circle which in truth rivaled the feast of Ali Şîr Nevâî, and from Ali Pasha Naima obtained heart-warming treatment befitting his scholarly attainments.*[58] *Thus when in* 1124 [*began February* 9, 1712] *the imperial army moved to Edirne, Naima was for a second time charged with the post of chief of the Anadolu accountant's bureau and then, when he had accompanied the army to Edirne, was made custodian of the register.*[59] *A few months later he received the post of chief of the head accountancy bureau.*[60] *As is set forth in the biography of the said grand vezir, Ali Pasha, Naima Efendi together with Habeşizade Rahmi Bey Efendi, Selim Efendi, the talented poet Sami Bey Efendi, and still other ulema-littérateurs, obtained the honor of being constantly overwhelmed in the sea of the said grand vezir's kindness.*[61] *When the conduct of the affairs of state was being discussed, the manner in which Naima would set forth the whole of his own experience and knowledge in all frankness and certainty and honesty caused him to be known as one who stood forth among his fellows.*

This prominence of the said Naima aroused in enmity the evil, sinister meanness of the nature of Moralı Köse İbrahim Agha, the steward of the said grand vezir.[62] *İbrahim Agha had a yellow skin and tiny eyes. He was short. His clothing was not clean. In society he was tedious. He had a sour face, blue eyes, and the offensive imperiousness of a malevolent disposition; a shallow understanding and a moral endowment of unbridled hypocrisy. İbrahim Agha set himself to deceits and to calumny against Naima, telling a number of falsehoods such as that Naima was using his proximity to the grand vezir as a means of embezzling and of getting bribes—things which are contrary to propriety—and also that Naima had dared to state publicly that matters which were being undertaken in connection with the approaching military campaign would have a disagreeable and an unsuitable outcome. Thus at the time when they started on the campaign, the said steward of the grand vezir in one way and another became the evil means and cause of turning the said grand vezir against Naima. İbrahim Agha left no opportunity for the unfortunate and accused Naima to prove his reliability. By means of these unadulterated calumnies, İbrahim Agha caused Naima to be betrayed.*[63] *He was transferred from the post of chief of the head accountancy bureau to that of* silihdar *secretary.*[64]

When they reached the Morea, the treacherous and sinister steward, having first made sure that the spoils which he had gained would be allotted solely to his own bureau, by malice and force had the said Naima reduced to the post of chief of the Anadolu accountant's bureau.[65]

Then when the army departed after the Morea had been conquered, Naima was left there with the title of deputy custodian of the register for the Morea. The breaths of his precious life came to their end in the Morea.

The said subject of this biography, Naima—God have mercy upon him—was a man of noble, praiseworthy traits. The first volume of the history which he was charged to write is the rough draft of the history which Şarih al-Manarzade had undertaken but had been unable to finish; this Naima collected and wrote out with a number of additions up to the middle of the year 1070 [*began September* 18, 1659].

Although Naima also recorded under the title of Volume Two the events from the said year 1070 *to* 1110, *he was not able to put this into final form and to make a book of it during his lifetime.*[66] *The said Şehrizade Efendi tells in his own little history how he collected Naima's rough draft and put it into final book form. Naima Efendi's grace of style and manner in poetry, in prose, and in the various scripts, and his correctness and rectitude and honesty in all the posts which he held are incontestable. God have mercy upon him!*

A number of points in the above account deserve further attention. They include the date of Naima's arrival in Istanbul (and the date of his birth), the nature of the halberdier corps in which he served while in the Palace, the tradition of his studies in Istanbul, the rank of bureau chief which he so frequently held, and the organization of the *kalem* or "men of the pen" career in which he passed his active life.

14. **Dates**

Tayyarzade's statement that Naima came to Istanbul "in the fullness of his youth" permits a somewhat more accurate estimate of Naima's age than has yet been reached. Certainly the statement cannot be taken to mean that Naima was more than twenty years old, and possibly he may have been closer to fifteen. At any rate, he had been in Istanbul for some time before the death of his early patron, Hüseyin Maanoğlu, which took place in 1102 [began October 5, 1690].[67] Thus Naima's arrival may have antedated the accession of Süleyman II who was enthroned on 2 Muharrem 1099/ November 8, 1687.[68] Certainly it does not permit one to fix Naima's birth any earlier than 1075/1665 at the most, ten years later than the usually accepted year.[69]

15. **Halberdiers**

As has been stated, Naima's post in the Palace service was, at that time, a very desirable appointment. The Palace body (*zümre*) to which he was formally attached was the *teberdaran-i saray-ı atik,* the halberdiers of the Old Palace. In origin this corps was a band of servant-guards, and it continued to perform its function.[70] But it had also come to include certain apprentice-secretaries; it was as one of these rather than as an actual halberdier that Naima served.

The Palace term of these apprentice-secretaries was occupied with work in the office of the chief black eunuch, the *darüssade agası*. He needed secretaries to assist him in his capacity of administrator of the imperial pious foundations (*evkaf* of Mekka and Medina), a position that emphasizes the importance of the role the Palace servants came to play in administration and finance, especially during the Women's Sultanate.[71] From their apprenticeships the halberdier-secretaries normally graduated into posts in the upper bracket of the state secretarial service, the *kalem,* as did Naima.[72] Certain halberdier-apprentices rose higher, to positions of the greatest importance and responsibility. This was particularly true during Naima's period. No less than three of the grand vezirs who play a part in the story of Naima's career were fellow-alumni of the halberdier corps: Kalaylıkoz Ahmed Pasha, a Kayseri boy who had owed his original appointment to a fellow-townsman in the halberdier corps; Baltacı (same as *teberdar*) Mehmed Pasha, originally appointed through a kinsman in the corps; and—most important of all (although he did not become grand vezir until after Naima's death)—Ahmed III's greatest supporter, İbrahim Pasha of Nevşehir.[73]

Any appointment as halberdier doubtless was rightly considered a worthwhile opportunity and the careers of two of the men named above are evidence that to be an apprentice-secretary in the corps was indeed an excellent start for a young man aspiring to a civilian career.[74] True halberdiers, in contrast to the apprentice-secretaries, might spend almost their entire lives in the corps as is shown by the following petition, dated about a decade before Naima was a member of the group. It was submitted by a halberdier of the Old Palace to Mehmed IV on 22 *Rebiyülâhır* 1079/September 29, 1668.

May God the praised and exalted make flawless the imperial being of my majestic, illustrious Padishah and prolong his life as the life of Noah! Amen. This his slave, being one of the halberdiers of the Old Palace and having worn out our life for this long a time in the imperial Palace and being now an aged man and old, it has been petitioned in the hope that the seven and one-half asper wage which I enjoy should revert to the treasury and that there should be graciously bestowed upon this his slave a sixty-asper müteferrika *grant. The rest is for my majestic Padishah to order and command.*[75]

At the top this petition is endorsed in the sultan's hand: "Let the wage revert to the treasury. I have given him a fifty-asper *müteferrika* grant."

Somewhat in contrast to such a regular halberdier, the apprentice-secretaries seem to have aspired to a standard of education and intellectual attainment, which, although more secular than that of the ulema, was probably not inferior to it.[76] In any event, reference to an Ottoman figure as a halberdier or—in the modern phrase—an "ax-man" (*baltacı*) should not be taken to mean that he was a hewer of imperial wood or a soldier who rose in the state service simply through his wit and his ability. At least some of those "ax-men" were among the most educated Muslim civil servants in the state. In all likelihood they, including Naima, would have been as unskillful with the halberd as they were skillful with the pen.

16. Koçi Bey

Mention should be made of the tradition that Naima studied at Istanbul under Koçi Bey, the author of the well-known *Risale*.[77] This is chronologically almost out of the question. Koçi Bey's dates are uncertain, but there is no doubt that he was an experienced, mature man during the reign of Murad IV (died 1640). Hence it is unlikely that Naima, who came to Istanbul only some half century later, knew Koçi Bey personally, all the more so since Naima seemingly made no mention of Koçi Bey when recording the chronicle of Murad IV's reign.

17. Rank of Bureau Chief

The "rank of bureau chief" which Naima received with his first appointment was the same rank as that attached to almost all of the positions he subsequently held.[78] In his professional career—that of the "men of the pen" (the *kalem*)—this was the broad upper bracket;

the next step higher would have been to the office of *defterdar* or else to a full-fledged vezirship.

By Naima's time the Ottoman word spelled *khwājeh,* "master" (from Persian: Ottoman here retains the persian plural *khwājegān*), but pronounced *hace* (plural *hacegân*) and so distinguished from *khwājeh,* "teacher" (pronounced *hoca*), had come in a specialized technical acceptance to designate an official of the top rank (*rütbe* or *paye*) of the state secretarial service (*kalem*).[79] The *hacegân* were thus a rank of secretaries. Secretary or scribe here, of course, is a very flexible term embracing all "writing" civil servants from the humblest account keeper to the most illustrious secretaries of the state.[80] No study yet made enables one to list with assurance all the officials who during a given period of the Ottoman state had the *hace* rank: apparent anomalies are not hard to find.[81]

In the present instance, Naima as secretary of the Istanbul divan had the *rank* but this particular post was perhaps not regularly a true bureau chieftainship. One finds a seeming parallel in the normal situation in which one of the Ottoman ulema could hold a relatively less important post but at the same time have the rank—*paye*—of a higher appointment.

As the secretary-service had developed, the *hacegân* became bureau chiefs in the treasury-chancellery. As such they eventually came to be ex officio members of the imperial divan and to be shown great deference on formal occasions. But, since they were appointed directly by the grand vezir, they should never be regarded simply as subordinates of the chief *defterdar* who, for that matter, was only the coordinator rather than the full administrative chief of the treasury-chancellery.[82]

Membership among the *hacegân* may not yet have carried with it a full place in the divan in Naima's time, but the *hacegân* did, of course, officially attend the sultan and they traveled, with their bureau personnel, in his train when he moved from city to city.[83]

The *hacegân,* although secretaries, were in no way subordinate to the official called the chief of the secretaries (*reisülküttab*). He originally headed the stenographic corps attached to the imperial divan, a corps that apparently had evolved quite independently of the treasury-chancellery organization in which the *hacegân* properly belonged. The *reisülküttab's* office in Naima's time was rapidly becoming an approximation of European ministry of foreign affairs while the *hacegân,* who presumably had originally developed from the secretary corps in the *kazasker's* divan, were regarded as part of the *defterdar's* "porte" although not entirely subordinate to the *defterdar.*[84]

18. The Kalem

Many parallels are to be seen between the *hacegân* and the ulema. Both the *alim* and the *hace* were born Muslims. This, indeed, seems to have been true of many of the Ottoman "men of the pen"—the civil administrators who followed the important *kalem* career—at all periods of Ottoman history.[85] The importance of the men of the *kalem* has been rather obscured by the overly rigid view that the developed Ottoman government under the dynasty fundamentally comprised only two "institutions," the one limited in its personnel to born Muslims and having religion and law (i.e., *din*) for its province while the second, termed the "Ruling Institution," was ideally composed only of slaves who had not been born Muslims, and had for its province secular administration (i.e., *devlet* affairs). In truth, even during the period from Mehmed II to Süleyman the Magnificent, the period in which a case for the two "institutions" can best be made, born Muslims were never, by any means, actually excluded from posts in the secular branch of the administration.[86]

The history of Ottoman institutions, particularly of the various organizations that were grouped under the loose collective term *kalem,* remains to be written. Meanwhile it should be remembered that the strength of the Ottoman Empire until well into its period of decline is more to be sought in an inherent flexibility of organization than in a rigid scheme of two institutions, and that there never was a time when the Ottoman "men of the pen" did not include born Muslims.

19. Dervish?

As has been stated, the account given in Section 13 is the best source of information of the life of Naima. Other sources to be cited in supplement to it only confirm and expand it, with few and unimportant exceptions. However, the judgments with which that account closes—that Naima was "a man of noble, praiseworthy traits" and "his correctness and rectitude and honesty in all the posts which he held are incontestable"—are those of Tayyarzade himself, judgments of a nineteenth-century writer who not only was exempt from the particular stresses and dissensions that had moved Naima and his contemporaries, but who also wrote in support of a later Ottoman thesis that the "Palace School" (i.e., the apprentice system) had been the basic factor in past Ottoman greatness.[87]

Naima and his contemporaries, living at a time when their state was in desperate straits, had moved through a maelstrom of conflicting personal ambitions and political views. In fact, we shall see that Naima died a virtual exile, that he was at least in political disgrace and that his honesty in office had been called into question. Much further study will be required before anyone can confidently discuss Ottoman "political parties" in the seventeenth century—if indeed the term "parties" is properly applicable at all—but one should accurately note two major factions which were in conflict throughout the seventeenth century (and for a long time thereafter) and attempt to discover where Naima stood in relation to this conflict. These factions may be called after the institutions which housed them, the *tekke* and the *medrese.*

The men of the *medrese* were the ulema, the organized corps of Doctors of Muslim Law who since the days of Sultan Süleyman the Magnificent had never ceased to be, as a group, a major contending force among the several groups seeking to gain that direct control of the state that successive sultans seldom sought to exercise personally. Despite their formal organization, the ulema were by no means all of one mind at any one period, and within the organization factions and schools of thought rose and fell as time passed. The preponderant trend was for the rigidly orthodox, fundamentalist ulema factions to forge to the front. Hence, in retrospect, it is all too easy to dismiss the ulema summarily as narrowminded bigots and to overlook the many liberal, patriotic, broadminded individuals whom the ulema corps always included. This misconception of the ulema is particularly easy because the opposing faction, the dervish orders, was largely a collection of secret societies about whom relatively little can be known. Except in the case of men who gave their lives to the orders, it is not overly common to find any record that a given figure actually was a member of one or another dervish order. Many of the ulema themselves were also members of dervish orders and this, in turn, was not normally publicized. The philosophic basis of the dervish orders was Sufism, Muslim mysticism. Since this Ottoman mysticism regularly had an unmistakable Shi'ite cast, it was particularly vulnerable to attack on the part of the stricter orthodox, for Shi'ism was synonymous, politically, with Persia, the great Muslim foe of the Ottomans. Hence Ottoman dervishes and dervish sympathizers had ample reason to resort, in the practice of their dervish-sufism, to the established Shi'ite principle of dissimulation. A modern parallel to their situation may be found in the recent practice of Free Masonry in places where it is highly unpopular or even legally forbidden.

During the seventeenth century there were two major occasions on which dervish-ulema friction not only rose well above the surface but even became the acknowledged major point of political discussion. The first was the "Affair of the Followers of Kadızade" (see Section 59) which was forcibly resolved by Mehmed Köprülü immediately upon his attainment of the grand vezirate. The second was the heyday of the ulema leader Mufti Feyzullah Efendi, the head of the faction that brought about the downfall of the fourth Köprülü grand vezir, Hüseyin, the patron of Naima. Feyzullah Efendi finally lost his life, and the ulema that particular opportunity to gain political control in the state, in the Edirne Revolt which brought Ahmed III to the throne (see Section 47).

Naima writes of both these events. The first he treats objectively as part of his chronicle. The second he treats less objectively for his account is part of a panegyric of Ahmed III, the sultan who reached the throne thanks to the failure of Feyzullah Efendi and his ulema supporters. In neither case does Naima specifically indicate that he himself is a member of or a sympathizer with a dervish order, nor is there any passage in the whole of Naima that clearly shows that its author was a dervish. On the other hand, Naima's janissary family probably had a connection with the *Bektaşî* dervish order, which was inextricably entwined with the janissary corps, and the same, of course, is equally true for the Köprülü family.[88] Throughout Naima's history, his personal opinions tend to put him on the side of the liberals. His scheme for the restoration of Ottoman fortunes has frequent Sufi overtones, as will be brought out in Section 42. His relationship with the Köprülü family may argue for dervish connections. The title that he gave the volume of history dedicated to Hüseyin Köprülü plainly implies that author and patron were linked by some dervish bond (see Section 22). His own name, Na'īma (in Arabic), is susceptible of a dervish interpretation (Section 23). Apart from these hints, there is the evidence of Salim, Naima's contemporary, which is the subject of the following section. On the basis of all this, it is to be concluded that Naima probably did have dervish connections and even that he was probably a *Bektaşî*.

20. **Salim's Life**

Salim Efendi, writing no more than five or six years after Naima's death, reflects the *tekke-medrese* differences and plainly regards Naima as a member or at least a supporter of the dervish faction.[89] It should be remarked that Salim's work is pervaded by the formal convention that every educated, successful Ottoman was, by nature, an accomplished poet. Only this convention explains Naima's appearance in a biographical dictionary of poets. His verse, like that of most of the "poets" in Salim's collection, had only an ephemeral value.[90]

From *Tezkere-i Salim,* 681–2 *The Historian Naima*

His name is Mustafa and he is from Aleppo the Grey. After he had harvested the capital of learning, he entered the body of the halberdiers of the Old Palace. Subsequently he was given a place in the group of secretaries and attached himself to one of the noble vezirs, Kalaylı Ahmed Pasha, obtaining the rank of divan secretary to that glorious vezir. Later, when the said Pasha became grand vezir, Naima enjoyed his protection and favor. Naima became a man of consequence and was honored with the post of chief of the Anadolu accountancy bureau. Thereafter he was at times out of favor and at times accepted. Still later he had a place in the circle of the Ali Pasha who fell at Varadin.[91] *Following that, Naima was nominated to the Morea where he died in* 1128 (1716).

Naima was a wonderful and astonishing poet of a quite unique sort. His own mortal mind continually summoned his imagination to the way of ease and rest, and his high position led him ever to embroider good reputations with the threads of good and evil surmise. Hence he always found it easy to cut the cloth of conjecture according to his own wishes. As a result, he considered himself the very spirit of the eternal chemistry of the crucible of learning, the full equal of the most choice judges of the court of the seemingly contradictory creeds of perfect decree.

He passed as talented in the art of literature and as able to fabricate Sufism if Sufism were wanting. He so claimed to be skillful that his behavior before the glass of pomp made it seem that he felt it was but a small affair artfully to corrupt and change the kaside-i hamriyye, *changing its meaning and altering it in one or another way without destroying its phrases.*[92]

Aside from this he evinced certain things in the various branches connected with magical knowledge as well as with the science of skill and chemistry. In sum, Naima was a witty scoundrel of a devil-may-care nature and a poet of broad doctrine. But he was skillful in his own branch of knowledge and an able writer of prose and verse. In the field of Ottoman histories his is perfect and detailed. He wrote much also—verse and prose, many a kaside, gazel, mukattaat, *and* muferrede.[93]

This composition is one of his works:

> Aşkımı efzun eden hat mı ya ol ibr midir?
> Zeynet-arayı çemenzar lale mi şibr midir?[94]

The cleverly spoken Naima, subject of this biographical notice, once saw a fine ihram *spread out in the house of one of the noble vezirs, a man greatly respected.*[95] *Naima instantly, on the very spot, had the audacity to ask for the* ihram *with this impromptu verse:*

> Safa-yı kalbla sa'yım bu ey destur-u saib-i nam;
> Merted-i asitanım eyleyim takbil ve istilâm.
> Harîm-i Kâba-i guyek tavafa eyledim zinet.
> Misal-i hacı üryanım inayet eyle bir ihram.[96]

Reduced to simple language, the important assertions of Salim, Naima's somewhat unsympathetic contemporary, are as follows:

1. *Naima was vain, gossipy, interested in matters (chemistry, astrology, etc.) which the stricter orthodox ulema condemned; he considered himself to be as good and as qualified to decide right and wrong as the ulema themselves.*

2. *Naima professed a "broad doctrine" and dealt in Sufism, i.e., probably belonged to a dervish order.*

3. *Naima was informal and audacious to the point of being ill-mannered.*[97]

4. *Naima was a good historian.*[98]

21. For Hüseyin Maanoğlu

The impression that Naima's writings make is quite at odds with that given by Salim Efendi. At the very least one feels that wide allowance must be made for prejudice and partisanship on Salim's part. A revealing passage, from this point of view, is the following section dealing with Maanoğlu and written at a time when Maanoğlu was dead and when no further favors could be expected from him. The section is Naima's account of how he came to compose his history for Hüseyin Köprülü.

From *Tarih-i* Naima, III, 179–80 (year 1043/began July 8, 1633).

Küçük Ahmed Pasha had captured the remarkable Druze Emir Fahreddin Maanoğlu-Fakhr al-Dīn al-Maʻni al-thāni *and his sons.*[99] *He sent the* fethname[100] *of the newly subdued Biqāʻ*[101] *together with Maanoğlu Fahreddin and his sons Hüseyin Bey and Mesud Bey, and also his large treasure, to the sublime threshold. The province of Damascus became obedient to him [Ahmed Pasha].*

This service of Ahmed Pasha was received with gratitude and he beheld imperial favor and bounty.

When Fahreddin and his two sons reached the imperial stirrup, he was imprisoned but his two sons who were sound and susceptible of being rightly trained were placed in the Galata Saray and enrolled in the number of the privy pages.[102]

Be it known that: the above mentioned Maanoğlu Hüseyin Bey later entered the privy chamber. By his natural abilities he quickly rose in the service and, in the earlier part of the reign of his Majesty the late Sultan Mehmed (IV) son of İbrahim Han, was privy secretary and a man well known and respected. Later on, after having served as steward of the imperial treasury he went forth from the Palace service. In late years, during the term of the late Köprülü Mehmed Pasha, he went on embassy to India and became an honored and important figure.[103]

He was endowed with long life. When he was an old man, I, the writer of this history, the humble Naima myself, had converse with him and was admitted to be a close confidant of his circle, a circle which was the pledge of honor.

In fact I heard from Hüseyin Maanoğlu's tongue and took down and have inserted into this history the real truth concerning most of the events which took place during the reigns of İbrahim Han and Mehmed Han (IV).[104] *As is proper, this will be indicated in the appropriate passages.*

The aforementioned dear friend [Hüseyin Maanoğlu] was a humble old man, generous and beloved, who combined in himself the virtues of wisdom, learning, wealth and fortune. He was a person of noble fame, the Barmecide of the age, the master of the five points of the sciences, understanding many strange secrets, dervish-like in his personal bearing, regal in his munificent gifts. His fame is enduring. Those who experienced his generosity, now, when something recalls to them the sort of a man he was, exclaim in amazement.[105]

He wrote an estimable book on symposia entitled the Discernment[106] *and he had this humble one [Naima] write out several copies of it. He presented one of these to the lofty presence of his Excellency Hüseyin Pasha, the famous grand vezir, the orderer of the structure of the peoples, the unerring guide, and the man who is the cause of the resurrection of this present history.*[107] *Thus Hüseyin Maanoğlu came to enjoy the incomparable bounty of Hüseyin Köprülü, that able chief. The truth is that the aforementioned book [Maanoğlu's* Discernment*] is a treasury full of jewels of wisdom, a peerless repository of marvels. He who beholds it receives an intimation of how perfectly instructed its author was.*

Maanoğlu Hüseyin died in 1102 *(began October* 5, 1690).[108] *May God the praised and exalted make his place to be the lofty gardens and cause him to attain the highest degrees!*

Were this poor one [Naima], in return for the admirable training which I enjoyed through the kindness he showed me and through his lavish gifts and generosity, for the rest of my life and with all my strength to sing the praises of his pure spirit, it would not suffice to requite the debt of gratitude I owe him.

His biography and an account of the dealings between him and myself I shall—God willing—mention among the events which are to be recounted under the year of his death.[109] *At this point, let us return to the subject. . . .*

22. **For Hüseyin Köprülü**

The above passage indicates that Naima had been taking notes for a history for some time before Maanoğlu's death (probably in the summer of 1691), but it was not until after Hüseyin Köprülü had become grand vezir (1697) that Naima actually began work on the *History* through which we know him today. The circumstances are related in the following passage, translated from the preface that Naima wrote in honor of Hüseyin Köprülü.

From *Tarih-i* Naima, Preface I, Vol. I, 8–12

To His Highness, Hüseyin Pasha

Grand vezir in the auspicious reign of the present occupant of the sultanate's throne and holder of the caliphate's office, Sultan Mustafa Han II, son of Sultan Mehmed Han IV, jewel of felicity's line, star of magnificence's heaven, fortunate khedive, mighty hakan, *glorious refuge of might, chief of the line of Osman—May God make his victory glorious and his glory eternal!*

[*Hüseyin Pasha*], *lofty presence, high exemplar, surety of the state, right hand of the sultanate, he who spreads forth principles of equity and mercy, who tightens the knots of compassion and justice, who brings order to the structure of the Ottoman kingdom, who forbids those matters which should be forbidden in the affairs of the kingdom, who achieves those things whose achievement is difficult, who composes the difficulties of the commonwealth, peerless vezir, resourceful leader who resolves all difficulties—May God strengthen him in matters of difficulty and shield him against seasons of dismissal:*

Verse [in Persian]

That good fortune which, with the revolutions of the passing years,
Shows forth the good tidings of glory and good chance
Does make the earth enslaved with its good creation
And does vivify the ways of honor and wisdom.

It is that prodigal of good works [Hüseyin Pasha], that lavisher of good deeds, that man of noble morality and fair nature and excellent character, that perfectly instructed vezir whose all-tranquil bosom is the treasure-house of wisdom and learning and whose lofty-disposed heart is the storehouse of truths and certainties.

Aware of the charm which the science of history possesses, his Excellency has ever been wont to have the finest books of this exalted science for the fellows and companions of the leisure hours of his days and nights. He has habitually refreshed his mind by investigating the wonders of the ages and sharpened his wits by midnight discussions of the accounts of the reigns [of the various sovereigns]. Indeed he so relishes reflectively tasting the sweets of narratives and noble deeds and has so completely assimilated the conclusions which are to be drawn from accounts and tales that, when mention is made of one of the important matters of the states and peoples, he will set that matter forth and explain it in detail [from memory]. Or if there be some reference to a deep significance in one of the ages of the tribes of Adam's sons, he will expound and set forth to perfection the difficult points contained therein.

In the courtyard of the fortune [of Hüseyin Pasha], that exemplary guide to virtues, the jewels of influence are without value and the gems of flattery carry no appeal. It was for this reason—since, as said the poet Ibn al-Muʿtazz:

Verse [in Arabic]

The gift of books is the surest way to the heart
of a man who counts his office as of less worth than is mankind.

—that his Excellency was presented with a most unusual historical compilation, an extraordinary rough-draft manuscript in the author's own handwriting.

One of the ulema, a certain Ahmed Efendi had undertaken the composition of a history in the "wondrous style."[110] *He wrote separate accounts, one by one, of the events which are reported in the Ottoman state*[111] *from the reign of the late Sultan Ahmed Han [I] to [the grand vezirate] of Köprülü Mehmed Pasha in the reign of Sultan Mehmed [IV].*[112] *He constructed his rough draft by taking [the account of] earlier events from the history of Hasanbeyzade and adding [to this what he wrote himself],*[113] *but before he was able to finish the composition—before he had constructed the final draft and written out the finished work—he died.*

During the following years that rough draft fell into the cupboard of oblivion, became extremely mixed up, and lacked little of disappearing entirely.

Now that writer [Ahmed Efendi Şarih al-Manarzade] was in truth an alert man, well instructed, a tireless investigator and a man of ready insight. Accordingly he was fully aware of the essential points of affairs and he understood the conclusions to be drawn from many a happening. Also, he wrote by topics, he appended comments, and he wrote plainly in normal language free from excessive rhetorical ornament.

His Excellency [Hüseyin Pasha], the master of the state, examined that penetrating composition from cover to cover, from the first to the last, and discovered for himself how much of understanding it embraced. Therefore in accord with the saying [in Arabic]:

> *A man is remembered for what he has done;*
> *Whatever has been useful has won its own thanks ere now.*

[Hüseyin Pasha] declared: "It is not seemly that a manuscript such as this, one which embraces so many deeds of the past, should be lost and destroyed." So he bestirred himself to procure for it a new lease on life. Prior to this time he had, with divine aid, completed many good works which perpetuate the excellence of his deeds. Now he gave his command, ever infallible, that this history be written out anew. And in accord with the verse [in Turkish]:

> *'Tis the name that makes chieftains to be esteemed;*
> *'Tis the die that gives shape to the silver and gold;*

he commanded his slave [me, Mustafa Naima],

> *The desirous of grace, the beseecher of the breast of the kind,*
> *The young and weak, the slave of exile, the friendless Naima*[114]

to undertake the task of arranging [the manuscript] and dividing it into chapters so that it would become another [new and separate work], one honored by his beloved name. Thus he gladdened [me] by employing [me] for this noble service.

Then this humble man (I, Naima) pursuant to his Excellency's command bared the forearm of meticulousness to write out the manuscript. I took pains to make [the work] complete, extracting from the standard histories whatever supplementary material was necessary for various passages and incorporating it [into the text].[115] *In addition I added and appended, right up to our own time, [accounts of] those events which have never been established as they should be.*

No effort has been spared to make it an eloquent offering [for Hüseyin Pasha], one which will include the whole of what took place and which will be richer than other histories.

In order that it might be signalized by his [Hüseyin Pasha's] precious name, it seemed proper to entitle it

> Ravzat el-Hüseyin fi hulâsât ahbâr el-hâfikayn
> The Garden of al-Hüseyin, being the choicest of news of the East and West.[116]

May God, the praised and exalted, make easy its composition, granting that it may be written and sealed in tranquility![117]

23. **Name**

The Persian verse quoted above indicates that Naima's original name was *Na'īm,* "one full of grace" (*ni'meh,* the grace and favor bestowed by God). Naima (Persian vocative form) is a *mahlas* (pseudonym, pen name, professional name, nickname) built from *Na'īm.* It may date from Aleppo but quite likely dates from Naima's days in the Palace system. Apparently the use of a *mahlas* was as characteristic of men in the *kalem* as it was of the poets and the ulema.[118] *Al-Na'īm* may have a Sufi-dervish connotation.

In Naima's case—and this was not unusual—the *mahlas* eventually entirely superseded the true given name, Mustafa. This given name also should be noted as possibly indicating a family connection with a dervish order. In an official document that mentions Naima's death,[119] he is referred to simply as "Naima Efendi."[119] In Arabic his full name would have been Mustafa ibn Ahmad ibn Ali al-Naʿīm al-Halabī.[120]

An interesting later parallel on the basis of which it might be held that Naima took his *mahlas* earlier in life than his service in the Palace is the passage in which Ahmed Cevdet Efendi describes how he came to get the *mahlas* "Cevdet":

"While still at Lofça [Lovech] I took the *mahlas* 'Vehbi' upon finishing lower school.[121] But in 1259 [1843] Fehim Efendi, saying that, in the past, two great poets had had the *mahlas* 'Vehbi' and that in comparison with their works a man's name and fame would suffer, gave me the *mahlas* 'Cevdet' and thenceforth I called myself by that *mahlas*."[122]

As in the case of Cevdet Efendi, so too in the case of Naima Efendi, the *mahlas* superseded the real given name in common usage.

24. **Largess**

To the information contained in Section 22, a passage in Raşid's history gives important additions. Raşid does not indisputably fix the date of Naima's presentation of Preface One to Köprülü; probably that had taken place some time before. But he shows that Hüseyin Köprülü's interest in Naima persisted till the end of his grand vezirate and that Naima was submitting his production to his patron, in sections, until Köprülü fell from power.

From *Tarih-i Raşid,* II, 533. 17 *Safer* 1114/July 16, 1702

Naima Efendi Receives Gift and Salary

Naima Efendi, who had been ordered to keep a written record of the events of the Sublime State, sent to the court by one of his own men several sections of the history which he was composing. In order to stimulate his ardor, the grand vezir, Hüseyin Pasha, graciously bestowed upon him a purse of aspers as well as a daily wage of 120 *aspers to be paid at the rate of three aspers to one* para *from the lease-revenues of the Istanbul customs.*[123]

Naima was further commanded to give all of his time in the future to the service which had been ordered. The said sum and the imperial patent for the said salary reached the official historian [vakayinüvis] *on the* 17*th day of the said month* [Safer]. *He felt new ardor for the completion of the said task.*

25. **Official Historian**

Raşid's assertion that Naima served as *vak'anüvis*, official historian, leads to a discussion of that office.

The Ottoman term occurs in two forms: *vak'anüvis*, "event-writer," and *vakayinüvis*, "events-writer." These forms have the same basic meaning—"recorder," "recording secretary," "keeper of the minutes." To the purist there is a shade of difference between the two: the compound with the singular, "event-writer," properly is restricted to the recording secretary who serves for one specific event (e.g., one meeting of a council) while the compound with the plural, "events-writer," should refer to a permanent recording secretary (e.g., of a standing committee).[124] This nicety in meaning was still understood and perhaps regularly observed in Raşid's time but it subsequently vanished. Modern Turkish usage retains only the compound with the singular, *vak'anüvis*. To attempt a clear-cut distinction between a class of Ottoman official recording secretaries and a group of official historians is futile.[125] To assume that every occurrence of the term *vak'a*- or *vakayi-nüvis* must mean "official historian" leads even further into error.[126]

Today one must allow for at least three possible connotations of "event-writer": (1) "recording secretary," (2) "official historian," and (3) "annalist" (nonscientific historian). The third meaning is of the twentieth century. It developed directly under western influence and need not concern us further. But what did "event(s)-writer" mean to Naima and to Raşid?

Naima does not use the expression, although other compounds in -*nüvis* do occur, infrequently, in his history.[127] One concludes that the use of -*nüvis* was a Persianism with which he was perfectly familiar but which he largely avoided in his desire to write a simple, unadorned language.[128]

Raşid, Naima's successor as "official historian," frequently uses the term *vakayinüvis*. One example occurred in the passage given in section 24, a particularly interesting example because, as will appear, the immediate source for this passage was likely Naima's own "daybook," where Naima had recorded his receipt of the patent (*berat*).

Other pertinent instances are found in Raşid's three prefaces and in his appended autobiographical note.[129] He frequently refers to himself as "official historian."[130] He also specifically asserts that Naima had preceded him in that post.[131]

Like Naima's, Raşid's original appointment (January-March 1714), was thanks to a grand vezir—to Damad Ali Pasha (Şehid Ali Pasha).[132] After that grand vezir's death, Raşid politely implied that the appointment had really been due to the initiative of Sultan Ahmed III.[133] This seems unlikely. Ahmed III had been sultan for almost ten years without appointing an official historian. He had appointed Raşid very soon after, and only after, Damad Ali became grand vezir. All appointments, of course, issued in the sultan's name and with his formal approval, but this was ordinarily only a matter of form. It probably was no more than that in the case of Raşid. Again like Naima, Raşid owed his continuing tenure of the official historian's post to a second grand vezir, in Raşid's case to İbrahim of Nevşehir.[134]

Hammer's assertion, based on a communication from his personal friend Abdülkadir Bey, that it was Mehmed Köprülü (died 1661) who appointed Raşid to be official historian and that this "fact" explains the short lacuna between the end of Naima's account and the point where Raşid begins is entirely unfounded.[135] It demonstrates how uncertain later Ottomans were about the office of official historian. It is also valuable to show how completely the educated Ottoman reader could neglect the elaborate preface of a book whose body he might know quite well.

A major difference between the careers of these two official historians was that Naima was a man of the *kalem,* continuing in that career while he held the historian's post and being paid, as we have seen, by grants from the customs revenue. Raşid, in contrast, was one of the ulema.[136] He continued in the ulema career, was regularly promoted from one to another titular ulema post while serving as official historian, and was paid in the usual ulema fashion—by an *arpalık,* the grant of the revenue of a piece of property.[137]

Raşid indicates that there had been a break between the end of Naima's tenure and the beginning of his own, Naima's appointment apparently having lapsed soon after the accession of Ahmed III.[138] Raşid also refers to early official historians of the Ottoman state, but fails to name any predecessor apart from Naima.[139] Beyond this, he implies that many previous official historians—apart from Naima—had not really been officially appointed at all but had written because they desired to.[140] His most important statement may be summarized as follows:[141]

> *It is astonishing that in the Ottoman state a regular official historian has not been specially appointed "for the purpose of fixing* [sabit, *to fix or record*] *events and happenings." Since no one has been employed to give his full time to this service, much of Ottoman history has been forgotten. From time to time an enlightened man, whether at a grand vezir's instigation or on his own initiative, has tried to keep a record of the events and reports of the ancestors, but since such writers were not official but "followed their own bent* [muhtar]," *the results have been unsatisfactory. Therefore it is plain that the sole means of forwarding the vital task of keeping a record of what happens in the state is for an individual to be appointed to give his full time to this service.*

When to this statement there is added (from the excerpt given in Section 22) Naima's assertion that he inserted into his account "those events which have never been established as they should be," one may be assured that prior to Naima there had been no real continuing line of official historians, however broadly "official historian" may be defined, and also that the expression "event(s)-writer" prior to Naima's and Raşid's time is more properly to be rendered as "recorder" or simply as "historian" than as "official historian" in the later sense.

Raşid's appointment was for the purpose of "writing out the events of the Sublime State" and the "service of recording events."[142] This recalls Naima's instructions "to keep a written record of the events of the Sublime State" (Section 24). These expressions show that their prime official duty was not to write the history of the past. It was to keep a day-by-day running record of the present. Hence Naima's "record of the events of the Sublime State," and the "history he was composing" were, in effect, two separate compositions although the former was eventually to be attached to the latter, once the gap between them had been filled.

Naima's calendar of contemporary events was a *ceride-i yevmiye,* a daybook kept from at least the beginning of Hüseyin Köprülü's grand vezirate, and probably begun "unofficially," that is, before Naima actually had been given a firman to write history.[143] One assumes that Naima continued to keep this gazette until early in the reign of Ahmed III. Later, when İbrahim of Nevşehir had Raşid go back and continue the account of Ottoman history from where Naima's formal history leaves off, Naima's daybook served Raşid as a source, and perhaps as his main source, for the period it covered. Raşid used it in Ahmed III's new library, a circumstance indicating that such a daybook was state property.[144] Eventual classification of the Ottoman archives will certainly uncover several, perhaps many, comparable daybooks. A comparable *defter* was being kept at least as early as 1001 (began October 8, 1592), but whether officially or unofficially is not absolutely clear.[145] Eventually this series of daybooks evolved into a true official gazette—Turkey's first official newspaper, the *Takvim-i Vekayi* (*Calendar of Events*), the direct ancestor on the Ottoman side of today's *Resmî Gazete* (*Official Gazette*).[146]

This evolution of the Ottoman *Official Gazette* from the event(s)-writer's daybook is distinct from the evolution of the idea of the Ottoman official historian. Here we see why the late Ottoman conception of the *vak'anüvis*'s office differed so strikingly from the office that Naima and Raşid held.[147] The later Ottomans—perhaps in a measure through western influence—came to feel that there should exist one unbroken chain of official Ottoman annals. This chain was to cover the whole span of Ottoman history, year by year, without gaps and without overlapping. The entire chain was to be printed.[148] Any author whose work fell in that chain was, by that fact, an "official historian," quite irrespective of whether he himself had ever kept an official (or unofficial) calendar of events, or even of whether he had used such calendars as sources.[149]

Recent writers have unwittingly projected this later concept backward in time. Searching for early "official historians," they have been misled into finding them in every "event(s)-writer" of whom they find mention.

The inconsistencies in the view that there had always been an "official historian" did not entirely escape the first Ottoman who compiled a collection of the lives of Ottoman historians. This was Karslızade who only as recently as 1259/1843 completed his *Ayine-i zurefa*.[150] Karslızade divided his work into three sections:

1. "Widely current histories," a catchall chapter, pp. 9–18.

2. "Histories not officially commissioned by the state," a distinction recalling Raşid's differentiation between official and unofficial, pp. 19–39.

3. Treatment of twenty-six authors of histories "officially commissioned" by the state, up to and including Mehmed Esad, the *vak'anüvis* at the time Karslızade was writing. These officially commissioned historians are grouped under two headings (pp. 39–78):

   a. *Şahnameciler,* authors of verse-chronicles entitled *şahname*s. Of these Karslızade can name four but can recount the lives of only two.

   b. *Vak'anüvisler*, of whom twenty-four are listed, Naima being the first and Raşid the next.

Karslızade's implication that there was a continuing official historian's office, known as the *şahnamecilik* up to 1000 A.H. and the *vakayinüvislik* thereafter, is an attempt to find order and continuity where there had been none.[151] It thus gainsays the good sense of the division that he had adopted. The same implication is in general carried over in Necip Asım Bey's later study on Ottoman historians.[152]

To understand the situation that Raşid envisioned when he called Naima an official historian, one must keep the following points in mind.

1. Naima's appointment as *vakayinüvis* may have been regarded at the time as the reinstitution of an official post—the keeping of an official daybook—which had lapsed. It may equally well have been conceived as an innovation of Hüseyin Köprülü's, but in that case it would have been only the creation of the post that was regarded as an innovation. The keeping of official calendars was a practice out of time immemorial in the Muslim world and in the Ottoman Empire.

2. Later Ottomans properly regarded Naima and Raşid as the first and second in the formal line of official historians.[153] But this concept of an unbroken chain of official histories matured only after the time of these two men—certainly later than Naima at the least—being consequent to the introduction of printing and that was achieved only during Raşid's lifetime.[154]

3. Of the histories of Naima and Raşid, only that portion that Raşid wrote at first hand (i.e. beginning with 1714) is a true *vakayinüvis* production in the old sense, a daybook or official gazette.

4. The official historian's post, beginning with Naima and Raşid, has no demonstrable direct connection with an earlier Ottoman institution aside from the fact that in Ottoman society, as in all other Muslim societies, the historian was frequently and even ordinarily rewarded by the sultan or another dignitary, and so was in this sense an "official" historian.

5. The grand vezir patrons of Naima and Raşid, at a time when the state was in serious straits, sought to turn the time-honored custom of a grand vezir's patronizing literature, including history, to an immediate, practical use, for they were convinced that a record of present and past events would aid in the task of repairing the fortunes of the state. Thus they had a share in the development of the final Ottoman concept of a line of official historians, a late (eighteenth-century) development.[155]

6. The mention of an official record of events at least as early as the first year of the second Muslim millennium is principally important because it increases the possibility that much of Ottoman historiography after 1000 A.H. may prove to rest largely upon such daybooks, that is upon contemporary or almost contemporary extracts from and résumés of Ottoman official documents.[156]

Today when an Ottoman historian is judged on the ground that he was or was not an official historian, the essential point, of course, is the supposition that the official historian endeavored to please official quarters and hence was afraid to tell the whole truth.[157] Doubtless this criticism is justly leveled at some of the later *vak'a-nüvisler,* but it is hard to see how it applies to Naima, at least to the extant portions of his history. The latest event treated in that history took place well before he himself was born. Aside from this, insofar as Naima's annals can be said to have a theme, that theme may be regarded as an attempt to set forth the errors of previous grand vezirs (and even to some degree, of previous sultans) in the belief that this record will enable the present heads of state to avoid similar mistakes. This concept of history is, of course, completely at variance with the gratuitous assumption that an official historian is afraid to tell the truth.

When in his preface Naima treats of contemporary affairs, he handles matters much more circumspectly than when writing of the past. This is understandable, especially when one recalls that Naima was—in the usual Muslim pattern—entirely dependent upon official patronage in his career as a professional writer. Even so, it is not possible to point to any passage in which Naima deliberately falsifies the record. Nor, especially when compared to his contemporaries, can he be accused properly of any overindulgence in flattery.

Thus the charges that are assumed in this derogatory connotation of "official historian" are not well founded in the case of Naima.

That he also wrote as an annalist is quite another matter, and when he is criticized as such (*vak'anüvis*), the charge is valid. To a greater or lesser degree his work displays all the limitations of the medieval chronicle. The fact remains that, to the best of his ability, Naima seems to have written honest history, writing always as a gentleman but showing remarkably little favor or partiality; and that this was the easier for him because he was writing of events long past rather than of the contemporary scene (see Section 62).

26. **For Moralı Hasan**

Hüseyin Köprülü, Naima's patron, had a relatively short grand vezirate, being dismissed in 1114/1702, very soon after Naima had received the recognition described in Section 24.[158] Köprülü and his supporters had foreseen his dismissal at least some months before it took place.[159] It is valid to say that Köprülü's failure to revitalize the Ottoman state, and that the like failure of Rami Mehmed after him were primarily due to opposition offered by the forces of ignorant bigotry, the more narrow ulema. But to portray the outstanding ulema figure of that time, Mufti Feyzullah Efendi, as the complete and sole personification of those forces—as Naima does in his second preface—is, of course, an oversimplification (see Section 47).

Naima's uneasiness before the approaching disaster to Hüseyin Köprülü and his supporters may account for the one note of personal discouragement to be found in all the *Tarih-i Naima.* Writing at about the time, Naima permits himself to say "If we succeed in completing this book. . . . (V, 347)."

In fact, little more than a year after Naima completed that volume, Hüseyin Köprülü was dead, Rami Mehmed had failed as grand vezir, their chief opponent Feyzullah after a short triumph had also failed and had paid for his mistakes with his life, a revolution had taken place, and a new sultan, Ahmed III, was on the throne.

Since Rami was well disposed to Naima, we may assume that Naima had retained his post as historian during Rami's grand vezirate and that he thus continued to keep his daybook until at least the late summer of 1703, the date of the Edirne Incident (i.e., uprising) which dislodged Rami and eventually enthroned Ahmed III.

Naima's whereabouts during this time are uncertain. He was probably at Istanbul, still keeping his gazette and writing on his history. If so, Raşid's account of Istanbul affairs during the Edirne Incident is largely Naima's own first-person account of what took place.

Our next clear glimpse of Naima comes in 1115–6/1703–4, the grand vezirate of Moralı Hasan, Ahmed III's brother-in-law and the first man whom the new sultan himself chose for grand vezir.[160] For this glimpse we turn to Naima's second preface, dedicated to Moralı Hasan, of which extracts follow:[161]

A. From *Tarih-i* Naima, VI, *appendix,* pp. 2–4
Section describing the circumstances in which Naima's "Volume II" was written[162]

This humble slave, Mustafa Naim the lowly, copied out from many pages of notes the history of the everlasting Ottoman state, adding thereto a number of noble lessons. He drew up and completed the work, and wrote out a pleasing manuscript. It was a work which collected all the events that had taken place between the date 982 [*began April* 23, 1574] *and the year* 1065 [*began November* 11, 1654]. *But, although various learned men have investigated the events and reports from that year to the present time, and have gradually recorded them insofar as they were acquainted with them, there has not been collected and written an organized history that includes the useful fine points and the helpful conclusions which are what one desires from history.*

Therefore it was resolved [*by me*] *to collect those numerous manuscripts and scattered pamphlets, to incorporate* [*in my work*] *the useful points which have been heard from reliable informants as well as those strange happenings which they have witnessed, and to compose and write out a good history comprising all the reports from the year* 1065 *until our own date—a history which, since it is to be appended to* [*my*] *first volume, is to be a heart-stealing book of the same entertaining and useful style* [*as that of the first volume*].

His Excellency the Grand Vezir Hüseyin Pasha who with his great kindness and bounteous gifts encouraged this humble slave [*Naima*] *to write the first volume, and so was the person responsible for so rare a work, is now dead.*

Shortly after his death, under the lofty guidance of the Presence of the Judge [*God*], *there appeared on the tables of existence a writing of a new sort, and the Feyzullah Efendi affair took place, accompanied by a general uprising.*[163] *But* [*God*], *His care for the future glory of the state, His Presence, the Cherisher—may His greatness be mighty!—He who makes elegant grace to show forth within every mighty form, caused his lofty command to be concerned with the renewal of the role of the sultanate: He brought to pass the ever auspicious accession to the throne of lofty fortune of his fortunate and inspiring Majesty, the Sultan son of the Sultan, Sultan Ahmed Han* (*III*) *son of Sultan Mehmed Han* (*IV*)*—may God make his glory to endure and strengthen his sultanate! And therefore when, as a result of imperial wisdom in administration, the flames of civil strife had begun to wane, the grand vezirate was honored by the moral qualities of the beloved person of His Excellency Hasan Pasha, leader understanding as Asaph, vezir resourceful in affairs. Then, in consequence of the blessings of the admirable measures taken by that experienced councilor, what remained of the effects of strife was entirely dispersed.*

His royal, divinely aided Excellency, Hasan Pasha the all-powerful vezir, had perused the former history [*i.e., Naima's first volume*]. *His own practical nature was pleased with its entertaining and useful points.*

Therefore he took measures to see that the final volume should also be put into final form. Upon his bestowing upon this humble slave [*Naima*] *command* [*to that effect*], *work was begun upon this task of arranging it and writing it out,* [*my*] *trust having been placed in God exalted. May God the great and high guard* [*me*] *from all obstacles and delays, and grant that it may be completed and written out in that style of wonders and in the heart-pleasing manner which are established in the page of the mind! Amen, oh thou Helper!*

B. From Naima, VI, *appendix,* pp. 54–8
Concluding section of the second preface

As is recorded in the preface to the preceding volume of this history,[164] *about the* 490*th year of the* hicra *era*[165] *weakness and discomposure came upon the kings of the Islamic state, and rebellion upon the order of the kingdom. In part this was due to the evil of the Mongol soldiery, in part to the base heathen, in part to lack of unity between the warrior classes and the administers of the state, and also to certain enmities between them. In consequence of all this, the Franks saw their opportunity and occupied the Mediterranean coast of the Arab world.*[166] *They took many provinces, as far even as noble Jerusalem, and they lacked little of gaining control of Egypt, Damascus, Aleppo, and—perhaps—even all of Arabia.*

But on the scene appeared King Ṣalāḥ al-Dīn, one of the Ayyūbid Kurds. Thanks to the blessings of the good measures he took, the Muslim state found its strength and regained those provinces from the heathen. At this time there was a man of affairs, one of the elders of the great ulema, a man whom they called Abu al-Najīb.[167] *Between him and King Ṣalāḥ al-Dīn there was a bond of affection comparable to that between father and son. He wrote a very special essay treating the management of the state and the secrets of the sultanate, and presented it to Ṣalāḥ al-Dīn, saying, "In every matter do as this tells you. And then, provided you are upright in your life, you will become such a world conqueror as was Alexander!" So he charged Ṣalāḥ al-Dīn who made this essay to be his life-preserver and ever acted in accord with it.*

When the late Ismetî Efendi undertook to write the history of the

Sublime State, he wrote at length and with many fine phrases.[168] *In his rough draft there is recorded in detail what had happened to this essay and how it had come into the possession of Sultan Selim. No formal history by Ismetî Efendi appeared after his death, but his rough draft came into the possession of the chief astronomer, that Ahmed Efendi who died at the Kaaba.*[169] *At least, so people say. At any rate, Ahmed Efendi did also undertake a detailed history. He himself, however, regretfully states that "Ismetî Efendi says that he, too, was eager to find this essay, but that it was not possible to locate it."*

In any case, [*Ṣalāḥ al-Dīn*] *became an independent padishah in* 567,[170] *his glory and his power increasing daily in strength. And it is the truth that he served religion and state in a way which has been granted to few other kings. Books of history are full to overflowing with honor and praise for that noble individual. About* 569,[171] *King Ṣalāḥ al-Dīn died.*

The aforesaid essay then fell into the hands of someone who realized its value and [*thus*] *disappeared from sight. Thereafter it passed from hand to hand and finally—before any copy had been made from the manuscript—came into the possession of Mu'eyyedi Abdurrahman Efendi, the retired kazasker of Rumeli who died in* 922.[172] *Abdurrahman Efendi had formed an exceptionally intimate friendship with Seyyid Ahmed Buharî, the court intimate who also died in* 922.[173] *In the course of their friendly, confidential discussions, the disorder and rebellion which occurred in the time of Sultan Bayezid happened to be mentioned.*

Abdurrahman Efendi produced the aforesaid essay and remarked, "If only there were some energetic official who would act in accord with these lessons and would be ready to put into practice what this essay contains!" They talked this over confidentially.

The honorable Emir Buharî advised him, "In our time there is one man of clear vision—Prince Selim Han[174]*—who would not disclose these secrets. Should you chance to be with him, you ought to convey to him this trust."*

Subsequently, when Prince Sultan Selim was on his way to his governorship of Trabzon, Abdurrahman Mu'eyyedi did happen to be with him. He brought the prince the greetings of the honorable Emir Buharî, adding, "My Prince! This cutting sword, this flashing light [*i.e., the essay*] *befits you. Your Highness already possesses those personal qualities which give you a right to the treasurer of these divine secrets," and he gave him the essay, the original manuscript written in Abu al-Najīb's own hand.*

Sultan Selim Han spent much time in studying it. He discussed it confidentially with Idris Bitlisli.[175] *As a matter of fact, the sultan's tutor, Halim Çelebi, to whom the essay was not disclosed, actually fell from the sultan's favor because he was overly curious, having once asked, in a discussion with Aya Idris, what essay this was.*[176]

Mevlâna Idris copied out this essay with his own hand. Some time ago this humble one [Naima] saw this copy in the possession of a certain man, but I studied it only briefly. The original manuscript is perhaps in the imperial treasury. If not, with a little effort it might be possible to locate it.

It is a vast treasure-house, but it is in Arabic. To be sure, the ulema and the katips *today read a thousand books of this sort, and understand the secrets which these books contain. But, since the control of affairs is not in their hands, this does not do one atom of good. On the other hand, if [this essay] were to be translated into Turkish*[177] *and to become known to the incumbent of the grand vezirate, it would do worlds of good. For a long time this humble one had prayed God that this matter might be brought to the attention of a resolute vezir who would have the essay found and would entrust its translation into Turkish to this loyal servant. It would be an important production, worthy for one copy to be preserved in the imperial treasury and another in the custody of the incumbent grand vezir.*

For, by God the great, not only does that short essay contain the lessons to be found in thousands of technical books—such as ethics-books, wisdom-compilations, histories, imperial letters, and kanunnameler*—but also it would put one in possession of a great number of hidden lessons and of weighty astonishment-provoking secrets. In short, it would be a work of self-evident usefulness and a beautiful treasury in which one could justly take pride.*

Now this essay is not the one which is commonly known as The Essay of Suhrawardi. This essay is concerned with the truths of ethics, economics, and political economy, and also with the verities of the difficulties which the state and the sultanate must face. In addition, it is an analysis of, and gives the conclusions to be drawn from, the secrets of the divinely granted tenure of the finite world. Under these five headings it expounds and applies essentials.

May God grant that it may be found!

As for the measures of reform which were mentioned previously in this preface, when people hear of them, they say, "But these are impossible things," and they do so because these proposals appear to be mutually contradictory.[178] *But if that great essay be found it will be perfectly plain that these perplexing questions really retain no difficulties.*

If the high efforts of His Excellency, the master of the state and the greatly merciful, Our Efendi [Grand Vezir Moralı Hasan] are aided, perhaps it may be possible to find it: then I shall endeavor gradually to translate it, at the same time continuing to write this history, and so I may perform a service worthy of thanks.

27. **Later Life**

The above is the final autobiographical passage to be found in Naima. From it, it appears that his situation at that time was not enviable. He was actively hunting patronage and he was uneasy enough to go almost to the limit of propriety in begging for official favor. There are several circumstances that indicate that in the year or two following the revolution of 1703 Naima found it impossible to reconsolidate his position that he might continue work as a full-time historian. Moralı Hasan's grand vezirate was short. The preface intended for Hasan Pasha is incomplete and therefore probably was never presented, in which case the grand vezirate must have ended before Naima had completed another section of his history. Finally, Naima's whole history reaches only to 1064 A.H., four years beyond the date he had reached before Ahmed III's succession, and the account of those four years is not a finished version but rather an incomplete draft.

It follows that Naima practically stopped writing in 1704. None of his extant work can be referred to any later date. This inference is strengthened by the fact that Salim, writing soon after Naima's death and about two decades after 1704, makes no reference to Naima as "official historian" but simply calls him one of the *hacegân*. Salim is perfectly familiar with Naima's *History,* but apparently in the intervening years it had almost been forgotten that Naima once had held the office which Salim now properly ascribes to Raşid.[179]

In 1704 Naima was still a comparatively young man—near the age of 40; he lived until 1716. During those last twelve years of his life he held a number of important appointments in the bureaucracy. It may be that he prized these posts, which carried much prestige, more than the post of official historian, and that he would not have chosen to return to his former work if this were possible. In any event, he did not. From 1704 on, we deal with Mustafa Naima the civil servant rather than Mustafa Naima the historian.

28. **Kalem Posts**

Between 1704 and 1716 Naima is stated to have held seven positions with three separate terms of office in one of them, as follows:

1. Chief of the Anadolu Accountant's Bureau (*Anadolu Muhasebecisi*), three terms

First term: The appointment was gained with the aid of İbrahim Nevşehir (later grand vezir) and was made by Kalaylıkoz Ahmed Pasha during his short first grand vezirate[180] (28 *Cemaziyelevvel to* 27 *Şaban* 1116/September 28 to December 25, 1704).[181] Naima was removed from office and banished to Gallipoli by the next grand vezir, Baltacı Mehmed Pasha.[182]

Second term: In 1124, before the army transferred from Istanbul to Edirne,[183] i.e., between *Muharrem,* 1124, and 9 *Zilkade* 1124/ February 9 and October 11, 1712,[184] Naima was again appointed to this post through the influence of Damad Ali Agha (later Pasha) who was not yet grand vezir but was already, in effect, governing the state. Naima retained the post until his appointment to be archivist (*defter emini*).

Third term: Naima was again appointed chief of the Anadolu accountant's bureau while in the Morea with Damad Ali Pasha's army and served until the pasha's return to the capital.[185] Thus this term of office fell between 24 *Cemaziyelâhır*[186] and 13 *Şaban,* 1127/ June 28 and October 11, 1715.[187]

2. Master of Ceremonies (*Teşrifatcı*)

3. Registrar for the Kalyons (*Kalyonlar Defterdarı*)[188]

The two positions of Master of Ceremonies and Registrar for the Kalyons were held simultaneously. Naima was recalled from his Gallipoli exile by Ali of Çorlu,[189] grand vezir from 19 *Muharrem*, 1118 to 18 *Rebiyülâhır* 1122/May 3, 1706 to June 16, 1710,[190] and presumably held these appointments until his second term as chief of the Anadolu accountant's bureau.

4. Chief Army Archivist (*Ordu Defter Emini*)[191]

Naima was appointed to this post after his arrival in Edirne (i.e., after October 1712),[192] and served as chief army archivist only a short time, being soon made chief of the head accountant's bureau.[193]

5. Chief of the Head Accountant's Bureau (*Baş Muhasebecisi*)

Naima was appointed in Edirne in late 1712 or early 1713 and served until March, 1715.[194]

6. Secretary to the Silihdar Agha

On 27 *Safer* 1127/March 3, 1715,[195] Naima was demoted from the office of head accountant and made secretary to the Silihdar Agha.[196] This was due to the steward of Ali of Çorlu, Köse İbrahim Agha, and occurred during the week in which Ali Pasha set out on the Morea campaign.

7. Deputy Archivist for the Morea

Naima was given this post when Ali of Çorlu left the Morea in the late summer of 1715, and he occupied it until his death.[197]

Of these seven posts, two—those of the *kalyonlar defterdarı* and the *ordu defter emini*—are not noted in von Hammer's *Staatsverfassung,* probably because they no longer existed in von Hammer's time. The other five were all *hacegân* posts, "*emin*-ships and *hace*-ships" in Raşid's phrase.[198]

Thus Naima's subsequent career was strictly that of a man of the pen. He never reached the top rank, a vezirate, but his appointments were almost all in the second rank. In modern terms we should say that he held a number of under-secretaryships.

Naima's date is still too early in Ottoman history to speak accurately of organized parties. His ups and downs are correctly portrayed, as shown in Section 13, as ultimately due to personal relations, good or bad, with the series of individuals who came successively to power, most of them as grand vezir.[199]

Naima's record in and out of office is not an unusually kaleidoscopic series of changes in fortune, but is entirely normal for the times. It was in this period—beginning roughly with the second failure at Vienna in 1683—that the men of the pen began formally to be the predominant element in the Ottoman government. The tendency became especially marked during the reign of Ahmed III. It is mentioned here to emphasize the importance of Naima's rank in the state service.

Raşid, who was himself present as official historian during the Morea campaign,[200] records in detail—but without naming Naima—the manipulations by which Köse İbrahim, Ali Pasha's steward, succeeded in getting control of a number of accounts which had hitherto been handled by the Anadolu accountancy bureau (to which Naima was soon to be appointed). İbrahim Agha did this through the device of a formal investigation, evidently well planned, which was held at Salonica, where the army encamped briefly on its march from Edirne to the Morea.[201] Naima was absent from the main body of the army at this time, on special assignment.[202] Perhaps İbrahim Agha had deliberately arranged this. At any rate, there was much bad blood between himself and Naima. Although İbrahim Agha was able completely to exclude Naima from Ali of Çorlu's favor, there is no reason to infer that Naima had been personally guilty, although he may have been so accused, of what men of the time would have considered mishandling of funds while in the various offices he held.

29. **Death**

For the last chapter of Naima's life we have the file copy, preserved in a *muhimme defteri* (proceedings of the imperial divan), of a firman of Ahmed III to the kapudan pasha (the grand admiral), dated the second decade of *Şevval* 1128/September 28–October 7, 1716, which dates Naima's death accurately and confirms that Naima remained deputy archivist for the Morea until he died. This document has been edited in modern Turkish transcription by

Ahmed Refik, from whose *Hicrî On Ikinci Asırda İstanbul Hayatı*, pp. 52–3, the following is taken:

Order to the Grand Admiral: Whereas my vezir and chief defterdar, Hacı Mehmed Pasha[203]*—May God exalted prolong his high station!—has communicated:*

(*a*) *that Naima Efendi,* defter emini *in the Morea region has died;*

(*b*) *that although the census lists for Morea province have now been drawn up by the defterhane and the* kalfa *whose* [*nomination*] *was* [*previously*] *ordered has now been nominated and his* defter *has been sent, still it is necessary that someone capable be* [*made*] defter emini *solely for the purpose of regulating the* [*Morean*] zaimler *and* timar-*holders;*

(*c*) *that Ahmed Efendi—may his glory increase!—the present* kalyonlar defterdarı *in the imperial fleet is in every way capable and skilled in the scribal art and will—God willing—be able to regulate the state of the aforesaid* zaimler *and* timar-*holders' affairs; and*

(*d*) *that therefore the registers dealing with the* kalyon levend*s are to be given over to the* kalyon kalfa *with thy* [*the grand admiral's*] *consent while the aforesaid Ahmed—may his glory increase!—is to take up his station in the Morea for this service:*

Therefore there has issued forth my all-glorious decree to the effect that thou are to have the registers for the kalyon levend*s given over to Hasan Hoca* [*the* kalyon kalfa] *and also to have the aforesaid Ahmed—may his glory increase!—ordered to serve as deputy* defter emini [*for the Morea*]. *I have been pleased to order. . . second decade of* Şevval, 1128.

This places Naima's death about September 1, 1716. He died and was buried at Old Patras. The cemetery has been destroyed, but what purports to be part of his epitaph has been preserved (note reference to "accountant" instead of "archivist"):[204]

Baş muhasebe mansibindan mazulen mora muhasebecisi iken vefat eden

"[Naima who] died as accountant for the Morea, having been dismissed from the office of chief accountant."

30. **Son**

The reader will have noted that biographical information concerning Naima is very incomplete. As in the case of many an Ottoman figure, we know nothing definite of the date of his birth, of his mother, his brothers and sisters—if he had any, his earlier education, his wife or wives, or his personal life. It is said that Naima had one son, Ramiz Efendi. He became one of the ulema, rising to be a *müderris* (professor in a *medrese*), and to him there is attributed an "excellent" *Tezkire-i şuara* (Biographical Dictionary of Poets).[205]

31. **Travels**

Autobiographical asides in Naima's history are naturally few, for that text breaks off well before the author's birth. The few asides which do occur are relatively unimportant. One passing reference to Ankara shows that Naima was there in 1105/1693–4.[206] Remarks concerning Diyarbekir may mean that Naima went on to that city from Ankara in this same year.[207] It was at the start of his career when he had been appointed secretary to Kalaylıkoz Ahmed Pasha while the pasha was deputy governor of Istanbul.[208] Probably Naima then accompanied Kalaylıkoz Ahmed to his next post, Diyarbekir.[209] In any event, Naima seems to have returned to Istanbul (where Hüseyin Köprülü had followed Kalaylıkoz Ahmed) before the pasha went on to still another post, Baghdad.

Other touches reflect Naima's boyhood memories of Aleppo.[210] Apart from Diyarbekir, Aleppo, and Ankara, Niama shows personal knowledge only of Istanbul,[211] Gallipoli,[212] and Edirne. To these places we may add no more than the Morea and the way there. Doubtless Naima regarded southern Greece, where he died in unpleasant exile, "a land of strangeness" in the old Muslim phrase. It is noteworthy that for a long-term successful Ottoman official of the period, Naima had seen astonishingly little of the empire. This is perhaps to be attributed to a somewhat sedentary, bookish disposition: perhaps it was simply "fate."

32. **Summary**

Mustafa Naima's life falls into three well-defined periods:

1. Childhood and young manhood: ca. 1665–1685. Naima was born and raised in Aleppo, a key city and—in terms of the Muslim world—an exceptionally cosmopolitan city of the Ottoman empire. He was the son of a locally important and prosperous janissary family. Evidently he had "advantages"—a good education, an easy entry into a career at the capital. One sees the many opportunities to meet important men and to learn at first hand which such a childhood would provide. Quite likely Naima was connected with a dervish order—presumably the Bektaşî order—and this circumstance would also have facilitated his entry into active life at the capital.

2. Earlier career at Istanbul, activity as a professional historian: ca. 1685–1704. Arrived at Istanbul, Naima spent some years in a formal apprenticeship in the Palace service. Already interested in history, he had entry into intellectual (and perhaps dervish) circles which led to friendship with Hüseyin Maanoğlu, to the patronage of two grand vezirs, and eventually to something of a departure from the normal *kalem* career. From about 1697, if not earlier, till 1704, Naima spent his life as a professional historian on an official salary and during this period he produced the history by which he is known today.

3. Later career in the *kalem:* 1704–1716. Events compelled Naima to forsake, or at least seriously to curtail, his work as an historian. Returning to the normal *kalem* career with its political hazards, he continued until his early death to serve the state in a series of important and honorable posts.

NOTES

1. Modern studies concerned with Naima's life are noted in *GOW*, 246 and *EI*, III, 839. See also the article on Naima in İA, IX, 44–9.

2. They have been overlooked in previous accounts of Naima's life. On the difficulty in finding biographical information on Ottoman historians who were not poets or members of the ulema, see *GOR*, IV, 598; compare P. Wittek's review of *GOW* in *Islam*, XX (1932), 197–8, 200.

3. Sultan İbrahim left Istanbul for an excursion to Edirne in August, 1644. Naima, IV, 80; *GOR*, V, 341. On Silihdar İbrahim Pasha, see Naima, IV, 105, 186. See also *SO*, I, 103.

4. Mir (=Amir) Assaf. Misread as "Osaf" by Hammer, *GOR*, V, 341. Compare Max von Oppenheim, *Die Beduinen*, I, 313. On Assaf's title "desert chief" (*çöl beyi, amir al-badiyah*; Naima later calls him "padishah of the desert"), see Oppenheim, I, 308. The title *çöl beyi* is still in use.

5. *Urban*. The *'urban-i bādiyah* of Naima, III, 64. See M. G. Demombynes, *La Syrie à l'epoque des mamelouks*, pp. 183, 219; and W. Björkman, *Beiträge zur Geschichte der Staatskanzlei im islamischen Agypten*, p. 128 (*'urbān al-ṭa'ah*).

6. *Ramīyah*, tax in addition to what the villages paid to the Ottoman government.

7. *Ukhūwah*, the sum extorted by the Bedouin for permitting a caravan to pass unmolested. Modern *khūwah*; see Philip K. Hitti, *History of the Arabs*, 2nd ed., 25.

8. A solemn formal meeting signifying that the emir recognized the sultan as his lord and the governor as the sultan's viceroy over him.

9. "Wild wolf"; judging from the name, probably a janissary figure.

10. Usual address of respect to any important person of a rank higher than the speaker's. See Deny, p. 62.

11. Name missing in all editions.

12. A *levend* was a member of the pasha's paid household troops, James W. Redhouse, *A Turkish and English Lexicon*, *s.v.* See also *OTD*, II, 358–9. An *iç-oğlan* was a young man serving (in theory, at least) an apprenticeship in the pasha's household preparatory to promotion to a more important post. (*) Whether the aghas had military commands or any military connection at all is not certain. Compare the aghas of Amasya city in 1642, all of whom were "worthy of being made pashas" according to Evliya Çelebi, *Seyahatname*, II, 189–90.

The governor's official retinue thus included representatives of regular Ottoman forces at Aleppo, but seems not to have included Ottoman feudal forces or members of the class of religious dignitaries. For a statement on the military forces that Aleppo could muster in the later 17th century, see Evliya Çelebi, IX, 368, *seq*.

13. Or "scarf"? the visible pledge of safe-conduct. See Oppenheim, I, 313.

14. *Devletlu:* an Ottoman official whose rank entitled him to the honorific salutation "Devletlu" (Your Excellency). See *OTD*, I, 438.

15. *Mataracı:* one who is in charge of the water-sack or cask and thus regularly one of the armed guard.

16. *Qūmāk* (colloquial Arabic, spelled out phonetically).

17. *Zilgayyat* (*dhi al-ghayyah*).

18. "Non-Ottomans," i.e., he did not league himself with open enemies of the sultan, whether the Persians or rebellious Ottoman vassals. Some years earlier one branch of the Beni abi Rish (Assaf's family) had openly supported the rebellious Druze Emir Fakhr al-Din II; see Oppenheim, I, 312–3.

19. On Bektaş Agha, see Section 10, above. He was the *kethuha* (*kahya*) bey or *kul kethudası*—one of the principal subordinates of the Janissary Agha at the time of Murad IV's conquest of Baghdad, and was put in command of the janissaries there immediately following the surrender of the city in December, 1638 (Naima, III, 379). At this time he was not *the* Janissary Agha as *GOR*, V, 255, would imply. The connection between Bektaş Agha and Assaf possibly dates from this campaign.

20. "Counted as obedient": i.e., among the *'urbān al-ṭa 'ah*.

"Abu Rish"- Emir Assaf's family. The ruling family of the Mawali tribe, then the leading group in the Syrian desert. See Oppenheim, I, 312, *seq*.

"Your band"- *ocak*.

21. Note the Shi'ite oath.

22. Second person singular.

23. Naima's own term for his home land is "the vilayet of Aleppo together with the lands of the Arabs," Naima, II, 175.

24. See Section 11.

25. See Zinkeisen, *Geschichte*, III, 247–60.

26. Cf. Naima, IV, 203, where the *peder-i aziz* who witnessed the sultan's insult to the grand vezir must be Naima's own father. In that case the chronicler referred to here is Naima himself and not his predecessor, Şarih al-Manarzade, to whom the term

is usually applied. Şarih al-Manarzade's father had died before this date. See Section 69, below.

27. "Wise": although the entire point of the story is that Hezarpare Ahmed Pasha was *not* a wise vezir, it does not follow that the adjective is used sarcastically here. It is a cliché which Naima, who frequently did not edit his source for inconsistencies, allowed to stand. Naima's own composition begins with the second paragraph.

Ocak aghas: the aghas of the Istanbul headquarters were the commanders of the empire-wide janissary organization. They are to be distinguished from the aghas of the Palace (the eunuchs) whose influence in affairs usually surpassed that of the janissary aghas.

"Purses": i.e., cash. One purse (*kise*) equalled 500 *kuruş*.

28. Messenger: *bakı kul*, "slave in waiting," one of the messenger-collectors attached to the financial offices. J. von Hammer, *Des Osmanischen Reiches Staatsverfassung und Staatsverwaltung*, II, 164–5.

Defterdar: the chief fiscal officer, through whom the grand vezir's demands for "contributions" were normally made.

29. *Kapanice*, fur-trimmed robe of state. *ODT*, II, 165–6.

30. The long, difficult Ottoman fight for Crete (1640–70) had begun in Sultan İbrahim's reign. By this time it was proving to be a costly and hazardous venture. In it the janissaries played a leading role, politically as well as militarily. Zinkeisen, IV, 730–1004.

The janissaries are represented as claiming their rights on grounds of religion (*din*) rather than those of secular law (*kanun*), and thus upon grounds that the sultan himself was powerless to alter, at least in theory. Compare Naima, VI, 240, where Vani Efendi justifies his conduct as religiously acceptable.

31. His life: Naima, IV, 31; V, 135–9. Compare *GOR*, V, 546; *SO*, II, 32.

32. Biographical sketches of Kara Murad, *SO*, IV, 356; Musliheddin, *SO*, IV, 496; Kara Çavuş, *SO*, IV, 392.

33. To the daughter of Kasım Agha, Naima, V, 138; compare *SO*, IV, 49. Musliheddin was also the son-in-law of an important janissary agha, Mimar Agha.

34. Compare Naima's statement on the relations between Kösem and the *ocak* aghas, Section 56 below.

35. Evliya Çelebi, the Ottoman traveler of the 17th century, customarily lists the janissary commander (*serdar*) of a *kaza* among its *ayan* (leading citizens). The others usually include the kadi, mufti, *kethuda-yeri* (local commander of the feudal forces), *nakibüleşraf*, the defterdars (if any), and the *dizdar* (castle warden). In 1082 (began May 10, 1671) Evliya Çelebi tabulates the following at Aleppo: an imperial defterdar (*mal defterdarı*, also called the *muhassıl*), a *defterdar kethudası*, a *defter emini*, a *çavuşlar kethudası*, a *çavuslar katibi*, a head translator, a *şah benderi*, a *sipah kethuda-yeri*, the janissary commander (possibly Naima's father), a janissary *çavuş*, a *dizdar*, as well as members of the ulema, the ayan, and the *eşraf*. Thus at the important commercial city of Aleppo there were agents of the imperial treasury and tax system and of the imperial corps of special messenger-guards (*çavuşlar*) as well as a full quota of local authorities. The older protocol of the empire is preserved in the addresses of imperial general orders (firmans) sent to all the officials of a province. Such an address names *beylerbeyis*, *beys*, kadis, *kethuda-yeris*, serdars, and "other ayan." For example, a firman of Sultan İbrahim, dated first decade of *Rebiyülevvel*, 1053 (May 20–9, 1643) in M. Çagatay Uluçay, *Saruhan'da Eşkiyalik ve Halk Hareketleri*, XVII. *Asırda*, p. 290; and a firman of Mehmed IV, dated 13 *Cemaziyelevvel*, 1092/May 31, 1681, in J. Grzegorzewski, *Z. Sidzyallatòw Rumelijskich Epoki Wyprawy Wiedenskiej, akta tureckie*, p. 5. On Aleppo in a later period, see Herbert L. Bodman, *Political Factions in Aleppo* 1760–1826.

36. Consult the material assembled by İsmail Hakkı Uzunçarşılı, *Osmanlı Devleti Teşkilatından Kapukulu Ocakları*, I, 318, 327–8.

37. *Ibid.*, I, 327, n. 5.

38. Tayyarzade, Ahmed Atâ, *Tarih-i Atâ*, 5 vols. (Istanbul 1291–3/1874–6). Mehmed Said Şehrizade died in 1764: see *GOW*, 295–8; compare Tayyarzade, *Tarih*, I, 158. In his review of *GOW* in *Ungarische Jahrbucher*, VIII (1928), 165, J. H. Mordtmann

states that one of Şehrizade's works has been published under the name of another author but gives no further information.

39. Apart from the "much else—verse and prose" which Salim attributes to Naima (Section 20 above), the only indication that Naima wrote anything in addition to the history and its prefaces is the note in *GOW*, 246, of a manuscript of "Political Essays" in the Esad Efendi library in Istanbul. This appears to rest solely upon an assertion in Bursalı Mehmed Tahir, *Osmanlı Müellifleri* (Istanbul, 1334–8/1915–9), III, 152. The manuscript was not available to Thomas.

40. No manuscript of this work has been located. The *unicum* listed in *GOW*, 295, if extant is no longer available.

41. *Haleb al-shahbā'*. See Demombynes, *Syrie*, p. 84, n. 2.

42. *Zumre*, corps, class.

43. Tayyarzade (*Tarih*, I, 206, 306) notes that apprentice-secretary halberdiers of the Old Palace studied at the Bayezid *medrese*, almost next door to their living quarters.

44. *Çıkmak:* graduated; the full term is *mansıba çıkmak*, "to go forth to an appointment," Naima, IV, 11. *Çıkmak* was a technical term applied to the formal ceremonial departure of an apprentice leaving the Palace service—or another state apprenticeship—to assume a fully responsible post. It marked the transition from student to graduate, from apprentice to master, from novice to adept; thus it had the overtones of school, of a guild investiture, and of a dervish initiation ceremony. Consult the materials collected in Albert H. Lybyer, *The Government of the Ottoman Empire in the Time of Suleyman the Magnificent*, p. 78; Uzunçarşılı, *Kapukulu Ocakları*, I, 336–8.

45. Official secretary paid and appointed by the state service. *İA*, III, 595–6. See also *EI*[2], II, 337–9. The divan in question was an important one. At this time Kalaylıkoz Ahmed was the grand vezir's deputy (*kaimakam*) in Istanbul (Mehmed Raşid, *Tarih-i Raşid*, II, 242–3), having assumed the post in 1105 (began September 2, 1693). Thus Naima's term in the Palace service was at least some five years long.

Kalaylıkoz Ahmed was so named because of his elaborate turban. A regular halberdier, he rose to become the Queen-Mother's coffee-bearer. From this post he "graduated" directly to be governor of various provinces, grand admiral, etc. He died in 1126/1714–15. Raşid, IV, 28–30; Tayyarzade, II, 145–6; *SO*, I, 237–8.

46. Rami Mehmed Pasha was *reisülküttab* from November, 1694, to February or March, 1697 (Raşid, II, 267, 387), and again throughout Hüseyin Köprülü's grand vezirate. He acted as Köprülü's principal delegate at the Karlowitz peace negotiations (1699), the event after which the *reisülküttab* may properly be termed a foreign minister in the European sense. Rami was a native of Istanbul, an outstanding man of the *kalem*, an educated, liberal supporter of learning and art. He became grand vezir shortly after Hüseyin Köprülü retired and held the post until the Edirne Rebellion of 1703. He is sometimes accused of having fomented that rising in an attempt to defeat the hostile forces that were paralyzing his efforts as they had those of Köprülü before him. Naima speaks highly of Rami but nowhere expresses any particular gratitude toward him. Since Naima did not hesitate to give full credit to those who aided him, one doubts that it really was Rami who secured the appointment as official historian for Naima. On this, however, see Ahmed Refik, *Alimler ve Sanatkârlar*, p. 258. On Rami see Raşid, III, 239–42, and Rifa'at A. Abou-El-Haj, "The Reisülküttab and Ottoman Diplomacy at Karlowitz" (unpublished dissertation, Princeton, 1963).

47. Hakımbaşızade Yahya Efendi, son of Halebi Salih Efendi, was an outspoken supporter of Hüseyin Köprülü, Raşid, III, 174–6. A generation older than Naima, Yahya had been born and raised in Aleppo, going from there to Istanbul with his father who became Mehmed IV's chief physician. Yahya himself was a doctor as well as one of the ulema. He was twice kazasker for Rumeli. Yahya, Rami, and Hüseyin Köprülü were united in opposition against Elmas Mehmed Pasha, Hüseyin Köprülü's predecessor as grand vezir.

48. He was paid from the revenue of the farmed Istanbul customs; Hammer, *Staatsverfassung*, I, 333–4.

49. Amcazade Hüseyin was the fourth Köprülü to serve as grand vezir. He was the nephew of Mehmed and cousin of Mehmed's sons Fazıl Ahmed and Mustafa. He was

grand vezir from 2 *Rebiyülevvel* 1109 to 11 *Rebiyülâhır* 1114/September 19, 1697, to September 4, 1702. See Section 25, above, on the office of official historian.

50. See Section 24 on largess.

51. Kalaylıkoz was grand vezir from 28 *Cemaziyelevvel* 1116 to 27 *Şaban* 1116/ September 28, 1704, to December 25, 1704, Raşid, III, 142, 165. Nevşehirli İbrahim Pasha, privy arms-bearer and son-in-law to Ahmed III; he was grand vezir from 1717 to 1730. Tavil Süleyman Agha, kızlar agası from 1116 (began May 6, 1704) to 1125 (began January 28, 1713). See the list in *SO*, IV, 725. Compare Section 15, above.

52. Anadolu muhasebecisi, a regular hacegân post, Hammer, *Staatsverfassung*, II, 148–9.

53. Baltacı Mehmed Pasha, twice grand vezir under Ahmed III, 1704–6, and 1710–11, Raşid, III, 165, 195, 335, 372. He is one of the most controversial Ottoman figures. His defense of his own policy and life is contained in a letter in his own hand to Ahmed III's mother, written shortly after the battle of the Pruth, Türkiye Cumhuriyeti, Kültür Bakanlığı, Topkapı Sarayı Müzesi, *Arşıv Kılavuzu*, I, document no. 10. See also Akdes Nimet Kurat, *Prut Seferi ve Barışı*, II, 187–91.

54. *Istirkab*, professional jealousy, professional enmity. Possibly an Ottoman coinage, found only in more recent dictionaries.

55. Çorlulu Ali Pasha was grand vezir from 1706 to 1710, Raşid, III, 195, 325. See also *EI*², I, 394, and *İA*, I, 326–7. "The martyr," *şehid*, is said of any Muslim who dies a violent death. See J. H. Mordtmann, "Miszellen," *Islam*, XII (1922), 223, 225; and Paul Wittek, *Das Fürstentum Mentesche*, p. 146, n. 1.

56. "At that time," that is, late 1118/spring to early summer of 1706. "Keeper of records for the Kalyons," see Section 28, above.

57. Silihdar Ali Pasha, frequently called Şehid Ali, was grand vezir from April, 1713, until his death at the battle of Peterwardein, August 5, 1716. *EI*², I, 395, and *İA*, I, 328–30. On the post of secretary to the sultan, see Hammer, *Staatsverfassung*, II, 41.

58. The allusions are to the extremely popular and respected fifteenth-century Chagatay Turkish poet Ali Sîr Nevâî, and his patron Hüseyin Baykara of Herat. On these two men see *İA*, I, 349–57.

59. Defter emini. Here it is not clear whether Naima was only custodian for the army or for the entire state. See Hammer, *Staatsverfassung*, II, 164.

60. Baş muhasebeci, a hacegân position. See Hammer, *Staatsverfassung*, II, 146–8.

61. Tayyarzade's notice on Silihdar Ali Pasha, II, 84–100. Habeşizade Abdurrahman (*mahlas*, Rahmi); Salim Efendi, *Tezkere-i Salim*, p. 280; Tayyarzade, II, 87. Selim Mehmed Efendi, see Raşid, IV, 183–4; compare with Salim, pp. 359–63. Sami Bey Efendi, perhaps the mufti Sami in *SO*, III, 7.

62. *SO*, I, 119.

63. *Mağdur*. This entire polemic may ultimately go back to Naima's pen.

64. Silihdar katibi, Hammer, *Staatsverfassung*, II, 50.

65. The army reached Corinth on 24 *Cemaziyelâhır*, 1127/June 28, 1715, Raşid, IV, 73.

66. On the time span covered by Naima's history, see Section 64 below.

67. See Section 21.

68. Ahmed Refik, *Alimler*, p. 256, fixes Naima's arrival *during* this reign (read *sani* for *salis*). See also Raşid, II, 157; compare with Naima, VI, 194, where it is plain that Naima was in Aleppo up until almost 1000 A.H.

69. See Refik, p. 256; Ali Canib, *Naima Tarihi*, p. 3. Also H. Duda, *Türkische Post*, Istanbul, III (1928), no. 324, p. 2; *EI*, III, 839; and *GOW*, 245–6.

70. See a register of 954/1547–8 cited in İsmail Hakkı Uzunçarşılı, *Osmanlı Devletinin Saray Teşkilatı*, p. 433.

71. Consult M. Fuad Köprülü, "Bizans Müesseselerinin Osmanlı Müesseselerine Tesiri Hakkında Bazı Mülahazalar," *Türk Hukuk ve Iktisat Tarihi Mecmuası*, I (1931), 210–11.

72. Tayyarzade, I, 305–8.

73. Raşid, IV, 28; Tayyarzade, III, 146.

74. For further information on the halberdiers see: Hammer, *Staatsverfassung*, II, 29, 45–50; Uzunçarşılı, *Saray, passim; İA*, II, 286–7.

75. The text is in Uzunçarşılı, *Saray*, p. 433, n. 3.

76. But compare the opinion of one of these ulema, Salim Efendi, Section 20, above. On the intellectual position of the *katip* in medieval Muslim civilization, see G. von Grunebaum, *Medieval Islam*, pp. 213, 227, 253. In Ottoman usage *ilmiye* and *kalemiye* were sometimes practically synonymous.

77. See *GOW*, 185, and *EI*, II, 1055. On Koçi Bey, see *GOW*, 184–5, 414; *İA*, VI, 832–5. See also Koçi Bey, *Koçi Bey Risalesi*, Ali Kemal Aksüt, ed. Kemakeş Kara Mustafa Pasha, "Kemankeş Kara Mustafa Pasa Lahiyası," Faik Reşat Unat, ed. *TTV*, I/6 (1942), 433–80, especially p. 445, notes 6 and 8.

78. *Hacelik rutbesile*, "with the rank of a haceship."

79. Consult Meninski, *Lexicon*, *s.v.*; A. Adnan Adıvar, *Tarih Boyunca İlim ve Din*, I, 88.

80. Consult A. T. Olmstead, *Jesus in the Light of History*, p. 178.

81. For example, the sultan's tutors who eventually came to be ranked as hacegân, *SO*, IV, 717.

82. Consult *GOR*, VII, 97; Hammer, *Staatsverfassung*, II, 161; Lybyer, *Government*, p. 167.

83. See *İA*, II, 174. For example, from Edirne to Istanbul in 1699, *GOR*, VII, 10.

84. *SO*, IV, 749. Hammer, *Staatsverfassung*, II, 137–89; for further information on the hacegân, see *İA*, I, 396–7; İsmail Hakkı Uzunçarşılı, *Osmanlı Devletinin Merkez ve Bahriye Teşkilatı*, pp. 63–9, 260–5. A complete scheme of hacegân posts in the early nineteenth century is found in M. D'Ohsson, *Tableau général de l'Empire ottoman*, VII, 191 *seq.*

85. For a later Ottoman view of the kalem career, see Mustafa Nuri Pasha, *Netayic el-vukuat*, II, 90–91; III, 75, 78.

86. One can easily find throughout the sixteenth and seventeenth centuries many men of Muslim descent who attained distinction in the kalem career. For a detailed study, see Norman Itzkowitz, "Eighteenth-Century Ottoman Realities," *Studia Islamica*, XVI (1962), 73–94.

87. Compare the study of Barnette Miller, *The Palace School of Muhammad the Conqueror.*

88. On the janissary-*Bektaşi* connection, see J. K. Birge, *The Bektashi Order of Dervishes.*

89. Mirzazade Mehmed Emin Salim, son of a şeyhülislâm and himself a high-ranking member of the ulema, finished his *Tezkere* in 1134 (began October 22, 1721). He died in 1152/1739, *SO*, III, 3; *GOW*, 272–3.

90. Compare Naima's verse on history, Section 60, below.

91. Peterwardein.

92. The wine-ode, an established genre of Muslim profane verse. The significance of the phrase here is obscure unless it be used as a generic term for Sufi poetry at large.

93. For these verse forms, see E. J. W. Gibb, *A History of Ottoman Poetry*, I, 79–87.

94. Such verse as this is virtually untranslatable. It depends for its point upon allusions and puns, and the puns in turn depend upon the allusive Sufi vocabulary. Not infrequently the full range of meaning is intended to be understood only by the full-fledged Sufi or dervish. The present verse may be partially rendered by:

Is it (the Real) that makes my love
(my beloved's downy beard)
(you cloud) ?
increase—or is it (that "pin")
Is it the tulip which makes the grass-plot
lovely, or is it the "tiny arc"?

95. *Ihram*, the special garment that the pilgrim wears while at Mekka. Also, "shawl," "throw," "gift of honor," and "testimonial."

96. In the second line *takbil* is read for *nakbil*. The point of the verse is Naima's cleverly unmannered audacity in soliciting the gift. Upper-class Ottomans were extremely proper in observation of a punctilious etiquette. Naima here breaks the rules with great finesse. The verse may be partially rendered as follows:

In plenty of heart my request is
this, oh! thou model statesman of deserved fame.
To embrace and occupy for myself all the
ill-fortune that awaits thee.
I have encircled and graced the
sacred enclosure of the Kaaba, the navel;
I am like a Pilgrim, naked. Bestow on
me a pilgrim's costume [or gift of honor].

97. In this, Naima conforms to the classic prototype of the jolly, irreverent, unconventional *Betkaşi*. Birge, *Bektashi Order*, p. 88.

98. The most rigid ulema at this time even condemned history as too secular. A. Adnan-Adıvar, *Ilim*, I, 139.

99. *SO*, I, 213. See Paolo Carali, *Fakhr al-Dın II Principe del Libano e la Corte di Toscana, 1605–1635*. See also *İA*, III, 665–80.

100. Victory-letter. Such documents are a regular feature of Ottoman official correspondence and of later Muslim official correspondence in general. See G. L. Lewis, "The Utility of Ottoman Fethanmes," in *Historians of the Middle East*, Bernard Lewis and P. M. Holt, eds. pp. 192–6.

101. Coole, Syria.

102. *Raşid*, sound in doctrine, uncorrupted by heresy, and capable of being rightly guided.

103. See Section 69.

104. See Section 70.

105. Exclaim "*vallahi*" and "*hayran*!"

106. *Temyiz*. No manuscript has been located. See *GOR*, V, 173, note b.

107. Hüseyin Köprülü was in command at Seddülbahir in the Dardanelles from 1689 until the spring of 1691. He then came to Istanbul as *kaimakam*; Raşid, II, 79. It was probably at this time that Maanoğlu presented him the manuscript in Naima's hand.

108. That is, only a few months after Köprülü's return to Istanbul from Seddülbahir.

109. The extant *Tarih-i Naima* does not reach this date. See Section 64.

110. Ahmed Efendi: Şarih al-Manarzade Ahmed; see Section 69. "Wondrous style": recording the *garaib* and the *acaib*, the "strange and wonderful."

111. *Memalik-i mahruse ve devlet-i aliye*, the well-protected provinces of the sublime state, the official title of the Ottoman "Empire."

112. See Section 64.

113. See Section 68.

114. The verse, in Persian, is by Naima. See Section 23.

115. "Standard histories." Alternative translations could be "current," or "universally accepted."

116. The title includes several Sufi-dervish allusions.

117. "Sealed": the allusion here is to the termination of the colophon of the presentation copy.

118. For examples about this time, one may consult Salim, *Tezkere*, pp. 331, 390.

119. See Section 29.

120. İsmail Pasha, *İzah al-meknun*, Şerefeddin Yaltkaya and Kilisli Rifat Bilge, eds. *s.v. rawdah.*

121. "*Yazmadan izin aldığımda*": "when I got permission," or certificate of discharge from lower school.

122. Quoted in Mardin, *Ahmet Cevdet Paşa*, p. 13, n. 14.

123. On the relationships between *kuruş*, *akçe*, and *para* over time, see *OTD*, II, 326–8.

124. Compare Wittek's review of J. H. Kramer's *Over de geschiedschrijving bij de osmaansche Turken* in *MOG*, I/4 (1922), 243–4.

125. Compare *GOR*, VII, 465 note d and *GOW*, 285, n. 1.

126. For example, F. Babinger, "Shejeh Bedr ed-din, der Sohn des Richters von Simaw," *Islam*, XI (1921), 5, and the references given there. Also, F. Babinger, "Ein türkischer Stiftungsbrief des Nerkesi vom Jahre 1029/1620," *MOG* I, 2–3 (1921–2), and *GOW*, 227, n. 3.

127. See Naima, II, 208; IV, 74; and VI, 125.

128. See Section 62.

129. Mehmed Raşid Efendi, died 1148/1735, *GOW*, 268–70. Author of the "official history" from 1071 (began September 6, 1660)—that is, from shortly after the point where Naima leaves off—to 1134 (began October 22, 1721), Raşid was appointed official historian in early 1126 (January to March, 1714). He wrote his history in three installments. In order of composition they are as follows:

1. The section from 1115/1703 to 1130/1717, comprising volumes three and four of *Tarih-i Naima*. The preface to this section is in III, 2–7.
2. The section from 1071/1660 to 1115/1703, comprising volumes one and two. The preface to this section is in I, 2–10.
3. The section from 1130/1717 to 1134/1721, comprising volume five. The preface to this section is in V, 2–6. An autobiographical section is in V, 449–54.

130. *Ibid.*, III, 6–7; V, 451.

131. *Ibid.*, V, 2.

132. *Ibid.*, V, 451.

133. *Ibid.*, I, 4–5.

134. *Ibid.*, I, 8–10; V, 5.

135. *GOR*, IX, *Schlussrede*, xxv, note a. Abdülkadir Bey Melek Mehmed Paşazade, died October 27, 1846, *SO*, III, 350.

136. At least on the upper levels it was almost unheard of for a man to change from one career to another. Cevdet Pasha asserts that up to the late nineteenth century only three men had risen from a *müderrislik* (ulema professorship) to become vezirs: Köprülüzade Fazil Ahmed, Osman Pasha of Yenişehir, and Şirvanizade Mehmed Rüşdü Pasha. Cevdet Pasha himself was the only man who had been transferred from the office of kazasker in the *ilmiye* career to the vezirate; Mardin, *Ahmed Cevdet Paşa*, pp. 51–61.

137. Raşid, V, 451. Compare Mustafa Nuri Pasha, *Netayic*, III, 77; *İA*, I, 592–3, II, 333. See also, *OTD*, I, 84–6.

138. Raşid, I, 6.

139. *Ibid.*, V, 3, 5.

140. *Ibid.*, V, 450–1.

141. *Ibid.*, I, 6–7.

142. *Ibid.*, III, 7; V, 449.

143. Raşid's only specific citation of Naima's daybook is dated 8 *Rebiyülevvel* 1109/ September 25, 1697, only six days after Köprülü's appointment; II, 417.

144. *Ibid.*, 449–54.

145. Selânikî, Mustafa Efendi, *Tarih-i Selânikî*, p. 338.

146. *EI*, IV, 945.

147. *İA*, I, 665–73.

148. See İbrahim Müteferrika's statements in his preface to Naima's History, I, 2–22 (separately paged), where his program of publication is to publish a series of history from Adam to his own time, using the best authors and stressing Muslim and Ottoman history.

149. *GOR*, IX, xxi, note a.

150. Karslızade Cemaleddin, *GOW*, 357. He is generally inadequate and unreliable. *Ayine-i zurefa*: edited and enlarged by Ahmed Cevdet as *Osmanli Tarih ve Müverrihleri.*

151. Karslızade, p. 39.

152. Necip Asım, "Osmanlı Tarih-nüvisleri ve Müverrihleri," *TOEM*, II (1327/1909–10), 425–35, 498–9.

153. *İA*, I, 671.

154. *GOR*, IV, v.

155. Compare Paul Wittek, *MOG*, I/4 (1922), 243–4; Mehmed Fuad Köprülü, "Anadolu Selcukluları tarihinin yerli kaynakları," *Belleten*, VII/27 (1943), 385–96.

156. Selânikî, *Tarih*, p. 338. Also see Section 75, below.

157. Compare Hammer's strictures on the official historians, *GOR*, IX, xxv, n. a. See also *EI*, *Supplement*, pp. 233–45.

158. Raşid, II, 539.

159. *Ibid.*, 540, the source is probably Naima's daybook.
160. From 7 *Recep* 1115 to 28 *Cemaziyelevvel* 1116/November 16, 1703 to September 28, 1704; Raşid, III, 99, 108, 140, 142.
161. Printed from the original manuscript (Naima, VI, appendix, p. 2) as a separately paged appendix to the final volume of Naima. Presumably it is copies of this preface that are reported from Cairo and Istanbul as works on the revolt of Feyzullah Efendi, *GOW*, 241, and Ludwig Forrer, "Handschriften osmanischer Historiker in Istanbul," *Islam*, XXVI (1940–42), 210.
162. Volume II: the section of *Tarih-i Naima* from 1065 A.H. on, Vol. VI of the six-volume edition. This second preface is incomplete. The opening invocation is missing, and the preface begins with this section.
163. On the Edirne Incident, see Section 46.
164. Naima, I, 31, *seq.*
165. Began December 19, 1096.
166. Franks: Western Europeans, Western Christians; here, the Crusaders.
167. Rector of the Nizamiyah academy at Baghdad; born 1097, died 1168 A.D. See A. J. Arberry, *The History of Sufism* (London, 1942), pp. 68 ff.
168. Ismetî Efendi does not appear in *SO* or *GOW*.
169. See *SO*, I, 239; the well-known historian Müneccimbaşı, *GOW*, 234–5.
170. Began September 5, 1171. Ṣalāḥ al-Dīn formally changed his allegiance from the Fatimids to the Abbasids in 1171, but did not proclaim himself independent until three years later. Compare Hitti, *History of the Arabs*, p. 646.
171. Began January 7, 1193.
172. Began February 2, 1516. See *SO*, III, 310.
173. *SO*, I, 195–6.
174. Sultan Selim I, 1512–20.
175. *GOW*, 45–9.
176. *SO*, I, 241.
177. *Lisan-i Türkî.*
178. For these proposals of Naima, see Section 48.
179. Salim, *Tezkere*, p. 261.
180. Tayyarzade, III, 36.
181. Raşid, II, 142, 165.
182. Tayyarzade, III, 37.
183. *Ibid.*
184. The date of the formal departure from Istanbul, Raşid, III, 388.
185. Tayyarzade, III, 38.
186. When the army reached Corinth, southward bound, Raşid, IV, 157–9.
187. When Ali Pasha was ordered back from the Morea; *ibid.*
188. *Kalyons*, larger sailing warships as distinguished from rowed warships, carried fighting men who came—at least in theory—from the feudal troops. Their accounts were kept in the *derya kalemleri*, Raşid, VI, 309. See also Uzunçarşılı, *Merkez*, pp. 422–5.
189. Tayyarzade, III, 37.
190. Raşid, III, 195, 325.
191. Chief army archivist, presumably deputed by the defter emini to accompany the army. The ultimate goal of Ali Pasha's campaign was to reincorporate the Morea into the Ottoman system and this entailed considerable activity in the *defterhane*. See Section 29.
192. Tayyarzade, III, 37.
193. The statement in Karslızade, *Ayine-i zurefa*, p. 43, that Naima became defter emini in *Recep* 1125/July 24–August 22, 1713, is incorrect and cannot stand against Raşid's contemporary note that Naima was demoted from the head accountant's bureau in March, 1715; IV, 35.
194. Tayyarzade, III, 37.
195. Raşid, IV, 35, 44.
196. Tayyarzade, III, 38.

197. The reconquest of the Morea entailed the reincorporation of that province into the Ottoman financial system after a break of some fifteen years, Raşid, IV, 114. Naima's role in that process is unclear.

198. Raşid, IV, 35.

199. The Ottoman technical term for the practice by which a younger or less important individual attached his fortunes to those of an older or more powerful official, whom he henceforth would support loyally through thick and thin, was *intisap*. For the individual with whom one held this relationship to come to power as grand vezir was the height of good fortune. On *intisap*, see the unpublished dissertation (Princeton, 1959) by Norman Itzkowitz, "Mehmed Raghib Pasha: The Making of an Ottoman Grand Vezir," pp. 79–85.

200. Raşid, IV, 45.

201. *Ibid.*, IV, 53.

202. *Ibid.*, IV, 48–9, 58.

203. Bakkaloğlu Sarı Mehmed Efendi who in this same month had been made vezir and was subsequently appointed governor of Salonika; *SO*, IV, 212.

204. Tahir, *Osmanlı Müellifleri*, III, 151.

205. Mentioned only by Tayyarzade, III, 38, 328. The date given there for Ramiz's death (1109/1697–8) is impossible, if Ramiz really was Naima's son.

206. Naima, III, 419.

207. *Ibid.*, 385–6, 388.

208. In early 1105/fall or winter of 1693; Raşid, II, 236.

209. *Ibid.*, II, 242–3.

210. Naima, II, 26, 136, 174–5.

211. *Ibid.*, VI, 249.

212. *Ibid.*, V, 70.

CHAPTER TWO
Ideas

33. **Introduction**

Although Naima eventually had wide experience in affairs of state, most of that experience came after his activity as an historian had ended. This does not mean that the ideas Naima advanced in his history betray inexperience, that they are overly dogmatic and would have been significantly revised had he been riper in years and experience before he came to write. On the contrary, it is closer to reality to regard his ideas as not uniquely or even primarily his own but rather those of his circle, and to look upon him as simply the medium through which that circle spoke.

These ideas can be ferreted out only by assembling the relatively few passages in which Naima speaks himself, in contrast to the bulk of his history where various sources are reproduced, for the most part practically verbatim. His interests center on two principal topics: government and history. Particularly in his two prefaces does Naima show us how deeply concerned he and like-minded men of the time were about these two matters. To understand what the liberal Ottoman of the late seventeenth and early eighteenth centuries felt about his government, about how it functioned and how it should function, and how he felt about history, how it should be written and why it should be written, we must examine those prefaces and then supplement them with the various asides interspersed by Naima throughout the text of the history proper.

34. **The Prefaces**

Preface One—the preface to Naima's own "volume one" (the first five volumes of the third edition)—in honor of and presented to Hüseyin Köprülü, is a skillful, elaborate defense of that statesman's policy while in the grand vezirate (Naima, I, 2–65).

Preface Two—the uncompleted preface written for Grand Vezir Moralı Hasan in 1703–4—is essentially a sincere courtier's defense of the conduct of Ahmed III and his brother-in-law, the new grand vezir, during the Edirne Incident in 1703 (VI, App. 2–58).

These two prefaces differ strikingly from the history proper. In the first place, they bear directly on Naima's own time. Within the bounds of etiquette, they are personal. They also, and this is especially true of Preface One, are more "literary" than the history itself; that is to say, their relatively elaborate style is closer to the involved prose that the period esteemed than is the text of the body of the chronicle.

35. **Preface One: Background**

In 1683, some years before Naima had come to Istanbul, the Ottomans for the second and last time in their history narrowly failed to take Vienna. Although the decline of the Ottoman state had started long before 1683, that date may usefully be taken as a major landmark in Ottoman history.[1] Prior to it, the Ottomans by and large either gained or at least held their own against Europe. After 1683, they were almost invariably on the defensive while Europe gained at their expense. The second Ottoman attack on Vienna in 1683 had been possible only after the restoration of the state which the first two Köprülü grand vezirs, Mehmed (1656–61) and his son Ahmed (1661–76), had achieved.[2] In a sense that attack, which was led by a Köprülü protégé, was a futile climax to their services to the state.

Europe pressed to take swift advantage of the failure at Vienna, and the Ottomans soon were losing heavily on all fronts—to Hapsburg forces along the Danube, to the Poles, to Venice in the Morea and the Mediterranean, and to the Russians in the Crimea.

The immediate Ottoman reply to this European aggression developed into a series of conflicts which the Ottomans called "the Fourteen Years' War."[3] Later Ottoman reactions to Europe's successes included the 1715 campaign in which Damad Ali Pasha (with Naima in his train) reconquered the Morea from Venice, as well as the earlier Pruth campaign in 1711. There Baltacı Mehmed Pasha defeated Peter the Great, but eventually contented himself with the restoration of Azov to the Ottomans.[4] The greatest Ottoman success in the Fourteen Years' War was gained by Mustafa Köprülü. Mehmed Köprülü's second son and the third Köprülü grand vezir (1689–91). His death in the field at the battle of Slankamen in 1691 was a heavy loss, although it is scarcely conceivable that he could really have restored Ottoman fortunes, even had he lived. Eventually the Fourteen Years' War was irrevocably lost, and the Ottomans had no alternative but to accept the fact and make peace for a time. This policy was unavoidable, but it was nonetheless unpopular, especially so among the rigidly orthodox Ottoman ulema who, at precisely this time, were almost at the very crest of their power.

Hüseyin Köprülü—Naima's patron—a nephew of Mehmed Köprülü,[5] and, after the death of Mustafa, the head of the Köprülü family, was a key leader of the liberal antiulema faction. He had openly opposed the course that led to the disastrous battle of Zanta (1697). His own ability and past record, as well as the prestige of his family name, made him the logical candidate to be that grand vezir who would undertake to make as good a peace as possible with Austria, Poland, Venice, and Russia.[6] He became grand vezir the day after Zanta and really negotiated the peace of Karlowitz (1699—the first substantial cession of territory by the Ottomans to European powers) and subsequent treaty with Russia.[7] Meantime he addressed himself to the equally indispensable and even less popular task of once again pursuing the minimum domestic reforms so that the Ottomans might again muster sufficient force to stand against Europe. Since Hüseyin Köprülü's foreign and domestic policies alike were unpopular with the large conservative majority of Ottomans, and indeed with all except the most farsighted of those who had the slightest vested interest in the Ottoman system, he met with determined opposition. This opposition, of course, was principally interested in furthering its own fortunes at home, and their criticism of Köprülü's handling of foreign affairs was, to that degree, rather a blind for domestic intrigue than bona fide conviction that the Ottomans could at once successfully fight Europe without prior reform at home.

These circumstances formed the immediate background against which Naima wrote his defense of Hüseyin Köprülü's course. His preface is a skillful propaganda document, nicely designed to disarm and perhaps to convert Köprülü's many critics and rivals.[8]

36. **Preface One: Structure**

The Structure of Naima's Essay *Pro Köprülü* is as follows:

I. Introductory Section (pp. 2–12).

A. Formal Invocation: Praises of God (p. 2), of Muhammad (pp. 2–3), and of his companions (pp. 3–4).

B. On History: its virtues (pp. 4–5) and its development (pp. 5–6).
Excursus: How to write History—Seven Principles (pp. 6–8).
Verse: To History (p. 8).

C. Dedication: to Köprülüzade Amcazade Hüseyin Pasha, grand vezir to Sultan Mustafa II (pp. 8–10).

D. On the inception, compilation, and title of the present work (pp. 10–12).

II. The Preface proper (pp. 12–65); full title of Preface (p. 12).

A. Foreword (pp. 12–26).

1. Naima's introductory remarks (pp. 12–13).

2. The Peace of Ḥudaybīyah, by Nabi (from his *zeyl* to the *Siyer* of Üveys (pp. 13–26).

3. Naima's concluding remarks (p. 26).

B. Section I (pp 27–44).

1. Based on the *Düstûrü'l-'amel* of Kâtip Çelebi (pp. 27–33).

2. The Five Principal Fixed Stages in [the Lives of] all States [based on Ibn Khaldûn's *Muqaddimah*] (pp. 33–40).

Excursus (pp 40–44).

C. Section II (pp. 44–58); full title (p. 44).

1. Circumstances Bearing on the Cowardice and Courage of Leaders, both in the Nomadic and the Settled Stages; also, the Disastrous Consequences of the Development of Luxury and Ease (pp. 44–6).
2. How Harsh Ministers Cause Despair and so Destroy the Capacity to Wage War (pp. 46–9).

Several Important Observations: Concerning the Circumstances of the Men of the Sword and the Pen (pp. 49–52).

Further Important Observations and Necessary Counsels (pp. 52–8).

D. Conclusion of the Discussion (pp. 58–65).

37. "The Means at Hand"

The outline illustrates how skillfully Naima's essay combines the highly developed Ottoman-Muslim preface with a telling propaganda-argument from history. This is apparent from the very start, even in the formal praise of Muhammad where, after the usual formulae honoring the Prophet for having proclaimed true religion and sacred law and for transmission of the Koran, Naima interpolates the following assertion, designed to show that Muhammad (like Hüseyin Köprülü) made use of "the means at hand," gathered loyal followers who helped him (as loyal Ottomans now should be supporting Köprülü), and was willing to subdue the enemy (compare Köprülü and his European foes) by a (temporary) peaceful settlement of difficulties as well as by the use of force.[9]

From Naima, I, 3

The tribes of the Arabs were a people hard to subdue, spirited to lead, and difficult to unite, but their natures were sound and unwarped, their moral disposition was free of that oversuppleness which attends sedentary life, and they were not stupid. Therefore that bearer of the secrets of prophecy (Muhammad), moving forward by using those possible means which arouse men to the task of summoning, undertook to guide and direct the wise men of the people and the great chiefs of the tribe.[10] *And there became obedient to his command those noble companions who, once they had donned the robes of Islam, came to grace the most august ranks. It was those renowned dignitaries, men promised paradise by the command of God, whom he summoned to serve him as his protectors and his army. And when, by reaffirming the right and banding together the hearts of courageous men, he had strengthened the temper of the association of helpers and companions, he then overcame certain of mankind through the word "accepted" and destroyed others with the unsheathed sword. Thus did that manifestation of complete greatness and beauty, the lord master (Muhammad), force into the necklace of submission the necks of his opponents.*

38. **Preface One: Foreword**

Of the balance of the introductory section of Preface One, the sections on history (section B and the excursus) are treated in Section 60, below, while the remaining sections (C and D) have been presented in Section 22.

The preface proper has a self-explanatory title (I, 12):

"This Preface Has Been Written
In a Foreword
Two Sections
and a Conclusion
For the Purpose of Showing How Important
It is to Make Armistices with Infidel
Kings and also to Make Peace with the
Christians of the Whole Earth, so that
the Lands [the Ottoman state] May be
Put into Order and the Inhabitants [the
Ottomans] May Have Respite."

Naima asserts in the foreword that among the gifts to man of God, the Healer and Ruler, is that he has taught mankind how to avail themselves of those courses of action which suit their own period and age of history. Also, he has ordained that in the world—between states and within individual states—there shall be now war and now peace, now contention and now union.

This is why Muhammad, although he possessed miraculous powers of which he could at any time have availed himself, accomplished his mission simply by using those practical, everyday means which were, and are, at hand. Muhammad thus, by his own precept, showed mankind the way to success. A striking example is the Peace of Ḥudaybīyah. Here Muhammad chose to make a treaty with his infidel opponents, although he could easily have smitten them with blows from heaven on high.

To emphasize this important narrative-parable, Naima reproduces in full a recent, highly esteemed version—that given by Nabi in his appendix to the *Siyer-i Nebevi.*[11] Naima then drives the point home by stressing that Muhammad's course was in no way dictated by necessity. Instead, he deliberately chose to make peace with non-Muslims as a means of teaching all the Muslims who were to live in years to come that there is a value in making concessions to one's foe and in making do with the means that are at hand (as Hüseyin Köprülü had done in adopting the necessary expedient of making peace with European powers).

From Naima I, 13-26, *The Peace of Ḥudaybīyah*

The holy imam and hatip, *Qastallāni, wrote as follows:*

One night in the sixth year of his sublime Hegira, [Muhammad] the prophet of God, that knower of royalty's realities and seer of majesty's minutiae, dreamed that he was walking as if across the earth's plain. Then he saw himself and the whole company of his fellow-exiles and helpers, and all of them were performing the religious rites [of the Mekkan pilgrimage], some encircling the sublime dwelling—God's personal sanctuary—others shaving their heads, and others hanging up their verse. Next morning, when [Muhammad] recounted to his noble companions what had taken place, they one and all became extremely happy and began—in the hope that this sun of conquests would that year enter the house of fulfillment—to do all that was needful for them to set out for the Kaaba. And although the tablet of [Muhammad's] sublime mind was devoid of any image of strife, nevertheless they reflected that there would be need for all swords in case the stubborn company of the Quraysh should bind together the rank of resistance: therefore each of them satisfied himself by taking with him his sharp-edged enemy-burner.

At the camp-station of Dhu al-khatīfah, [Muhammad] covered, girded, and marked seventy head of sacrificial beasts, to set them apart, while the other monotheists [that is, Muhammad's Muslim companions] also, as they were able, girded and marked their sacrificial beasts in the wonted manner.

While the emperor of apostleship's retinue—upon him the beautiful of salutation!—was passing by the place called Thanīyat al-Mazār, his personal steed, the crop-eared she-camel, put the four-legged chair of the body flat to the ground—although she had not been ordered to kneel nor had any sign been given—and stayed fixed upon the ground-nest. They came from all sides to make her rise and go on, but she all the more let loose the rope of strength. The faithful companions round about the stirrup of fortune's resort therefore said, "'Tis likely that the she-camel's strength and power have been abraded by the hand of powerlessness."

Then his honor [Muhammad], signet-knower of the device of whatsoever is real—upon him the finest of salutations!—said, "That the shank of the she-camel's power should become bound rider of weakness and impotency is not worthy of belief. Perhaps his honor, the Lord of the worlds, he who with flights of birds made an aerial barrier withstanding the masters of the elephant's resolution to visit the Kaaba, now again—as an admonishment—has put the halter-rope of a time of waiting to the she-camel's foot of intention, and does not give permission [for us] to go on to the sublime Kaaba's side."

When he had moved his lips in wisdom-proportioned answer, they accordingly bound the circle of the tents of rest at the place called Ḥudaybīyah, round about an almost dried-up well.

The fifth fascicle of the Istanbul catalogue is devoted to the manuscripts of Ottoman *siyer* works extant in Istanbul today. It demonstrates how extremely popular this literature became. Ottoman *siyer* was principally translated from, or based on, Persian versions, but translations directly from Arabic were not uncommon. *Siyer* literature treats of Muhammad's "way" or sunnah. In its simpler forms it blends into folk-tales. In earlier Ottoman times such tales had been incorporated in what has proven to be the most enduringly popular of all Ottoman poetry, Süleyman Çelebi's *Mevlid-i şerif.*[12] The more sophisticated Ottoman *siyer* literature, represented by Nabi, developed much later, chiefly between 1600 and 1750. A century after the deaths of Naima and Nabi, the Ottoman historian Asim was translating and writing a commentary on *siyer.* He proposed to write "In a different way from Veysi and Nabi, in a style from which all can profit. . . ."[13] It is a paradox that Nabi's *siyer* should be at one time both so difficult that even the educated reader could understand it only with the help of dictionary and commentary, yet also so popular that Naima would take the opportunity to quote from it at length. Such, however, was the case. A partial explanation may be found in the fact that the ordinary Ottoman "reader" frequently *heard* such literature read aloud by a professional and did not read it himself from the manuscript.

39. From the Düstûrü'l-'amel

Of the two parts of Section One, the first is based on Kâtip Çelebi's *Düstûrü'l-'amel.*[14] At the end of this part Naima states that his main points are chosen from what Kâtip Çelebi has to say, but are arranged in a new order and implemented with other useful points (I, 33).

The *Düstûrü'l-'amel* (Guide to Practice) is perhaps the best as well as the best known of the many Ottoman treatments of how to check the decay of the Ottoman state.[15] It was written by Kâtip Çelebi (Hacı Halife)[16] soon after an emergency council on state finance which that great Ottoman scholar himself had attended on 19 *Rebiyülâhır* 1603/March 19, 1653, and is really not a book but a confidential memorandum intended only for private circulation among a small group of influential persons. Kâtip Çelebi's recommendations were drawn up thus: *first,* a succinct analysis of the plight of the Anatolian peasants, a subject which he knew at first hand; *second,* a presentation of statistics on the size and cost of the Ottoman military establishment from the time of Süleyman I to the author's day; *third,* a review of the Ottoman fiscal deficit, 972/1564 to date. Then, coming swiftly to the point, Kâtip Çelebi analyzes the present position. There are a number of measures that could conceivably be taken, but which seem unlikely to be feasible in the near future: these include the coming of a dictator, a man of the sword, who would enforce the necessary reforms;[17] or else some group initiative on the part of the sultan's vezirs, of the military, or even of those two groups in combination. In contrast to these measures are others that can and should be taken at once: these comprise a series of financial reforms, reforms in the *kalem* bureaus in which Kâtip Çelebi spent much of his life as a subordinate, and in which Naima was to make his career as an administrator. Kâtip Çelebi concludes his memorandum with a charming note of encouragement. The Ottomans must not despair. They have weathered wars of succession, Timur's attack, and the great *Celâlî* civil struggles in Anatolia (see Section 65). Through it all, good management has always mended affairs and will do so again. The new sultan is increasing in power and felicity.[18] Let his vezirs labor for the faith and for the state. God will help them overcome all foes, and the Ottoman order will again win its way back to the *kanun* (that is, to the way things should be).

Kâtip Çelebi made this remarkably effective memorandum doubly telling by setting it into a familiar, meaningful frame—the analogy between the body, the equilibrium of its four humors, and its health on the one hand and the state, the equilibrium between its four component classes, and its well-being on the other.

It is only this frame, and not the facts and conclusions of the *Düstûrü'l-'amel* that Naima appropriates. Thus in one sense he takes only the rind of Kâtip Çelebi's composition, and casts away the meat of the fruit itself. But Naima was writing a half century after Kâtip Çelebi. In the meantime the man of the sword, Mehmed Köprülü, and his successors had "restored the state" with a degree of success which probably even surpassed Kâtip Çelebi's hopes, but after 1683 fresh disasters had reduced the Ottomans to a sorrier plight than that of the *Düstûrü'l-'amel*'s day. Hence it was not Kâtip Çelebi's outdated facts and figures that Naima could use with effect, but rather the prestige of the *Düstûr* and of its author. The correspondence of this section of Naima's *Preface One* and of Kâtip Çelebi's *Düstûrü'l-'amel* is as follows:

Düstûr, pp. 119–39	Naima, I, 27–33
pp. 119–22 (Author's preface)	
p. 122, line 4 on (Introduction) Man, his four humors, and the three ages of his life. These correspond to the state, its four components, and the three ages of its life.[19]	

Düstûr, pp. 119–39	Naima, I, 27–33
pp. 124–29 (Part I) On the condition of the peasants (*raiyyet*):	
A. The peasants and their function in the state correspond to the spleen and its function in the body.	I, 27–29, verbatim.
B. Historic policies of the Ottoman state in dealing with its peasants. The peasants' present condition, its cause, and its cure. (p. 126, line 17 to p. 129, line 11)	Naima further develops the analogy between the spleen and the peasantry, then discusses the bile and the merchant (*tuccar*) class.
pp. 129–33 (Part II) On the condition of the military (*asker*) class:	
A. The military and their function in the state correspond to the phlegm and its function in the body. (p. 129, line 12 to p. 130, line 18)	I, 30, lines 5–31, verbatim
B. Statistics on the Ottoman army, Süleyman I to date. Recommended cure for present conditions. (p. 130, line 18 to p. 135, line 5)	
pp. 133–36 (Part III) On the condition of the treasury (*hazine*):	

Düstûr, pp. 119–39	Naima, I, 27–33
A. The treasury, *defterdars* and *katips* and their functions in the state, corresponds to the stomach and the digestive powers and to their functions in the body.	I, 30, line 22 to I, 31, line 8, verbatim
B. Statistics on Ottoman deficits, 972/1564 to date. Causes and cures.	
pp. 136–9 (Conclusion)	
A. Cures "possible" but not likely to be realized soon.	
B. Practical measures to be taken at once.	Only one echo; Naima, I, 54.
C. A word of admonition and encouragement.	

The remainder of the first part of Naima's Section One is given to a further development of the analogy between the life and health of man and the life and condition of the state. Extinction is not the immediately inevitable end of an "old" state (such as the Ottoman), provided that a skillful physician (that is, Hüseyin Köprülü) be at hand.

The one indispensable condition governing such a physician's success is policy (*siyaset*), and of policy there are two sorts, that designed by human minds (*aklî*) and that set forth for Islam by God (*Şer'î*). Naturally, Christian rulers can avail themselves only of the former, an inferior kind of policy, and this fact is a source of legitimate hope for those who are interested in the fortunes of the Muslim [Ottoman] state.

40. "The Ages of the State"

In part two of Section One Naima outlines the five principal fixed stages in the lives of all states (I, 33–40):[20]

1. The heroic age, in which the new state breaks away from the fragments of the preceding state. It is in this stage that the permanency of the state's glory and fortune is either won or lost.

2. The stage in which the dynasty with its slave-servants consolidates its position. This is the stage of personal rule in which the ruler eliminates those elements which, in stage one, had assisted him almost as his equals.

3. The stage of confident security. It is the heyday of the men of the pen.

4. The stage of contentment or surfeit, when desire fails and men are wholly content with what they have, not bestirring themselves to gain more. This stage is the heyday of deputies and dignitaries, and is marked by a tendency for men to live in the past.

5. The stage of disintegration, dissipation, and extravagance, marked by outlandish and ineffective innovations.

In his exposition of these five stages, Naima inserts only one important personal interpretation concerning his own state (I, 36): In the case of the Ottoman state, it has been particularly true that the professional organizations of its "slaves," that is, the men of the sword, of the pen, etc., both their elite and their commonality, have come to be of widely different sorts. The training, etiquette, special clothing, and practices peculiar to each company of these "slave organizations" have ramified into mutually different and distinct codes and regulations. This is fortunate, for it has meant that the state retains the loyalty of all, a circumstance not found in less happy states. Hence, although most states perish in stage two, because the ruler is not able to subdue all his former helpers who now wish to prevent him from exercising absolute power, this did not prove to be the case in Ottoman history.

Another major point (I, 59) in Naima's exposition of the five stages of the state is his judgment that during the grand vezirate of Kara Mustafa Pasha (at the time of the second failure at Vienna,

1683), the Ottoman state had reached its fourth stage, the time of laxness and lethargy (from which Hüseyin Köprülü is arousing it).

41. "Circle of Equity"

The final section of the foreword opens with a "circle of equity" (I, 40–44). Naima attributes this to Kınalızade Ali Efendi's well-known *Ahlak-ı Alâî*[21] which, in turn, had taken it from Ibn Khaldûn. The parts of this "circle" (they should be written one after the other, entirely around the circumference of an unbroken circle) are as follows:

1. There is no *mulk* and no *devlet* without the military and without man-power.[22]

2. Men are to be found only by means of wealth (*mal*).

3. Wealth is only to be garnered from the peasantry.

4. The peasantry is to be maintained in prosperity only through justice.

5. And without *mulk* and *devlet* there can be no justice. The circle serves, of course, to point up the absolute necessity of Hüseyin Köprülü's domestic reforms if the Ottoman state is again to reach a degree of power adequate to withstand its European foes.

42. Ṣalāḥ al-Dīn and Köprülü

Following this, Naima notes that some authorities hold that the decline of the state is also a circle, a vicious circle, and cannot be arrested. Against this is the view of Maqrīsi who, in his *Sulūk,* describes how the Franks (the Crusaders) took Syria.[23] Most of these Franks were *Nemçe* (Austrians and Germans), the subjects of an emperor. They even compelled the Muslims to surrender Jerusalem. But, in the end, Ṣalāḥ al-Dīn (cf. Köprülü) was able to restore the situation completely.

Naima adds that 'Abd al-Rahmān al-Shirāzi's book[24] is a first-hand account of the manner in which Ṣalāḥ al-Dīn achieved his goal. Âli, in his *Nasihatü's-Selâtin,*[25] has translated certain of Shirāzi's valuable points into Ottoman, and Naima has abridged them and appended them to this preface as a separate essay.

There is no evidence to connect Naima's somewhat surprising

analogy between Ṣalāḥ al-Dīn's problem and the problem of the Ottomans after 1683 with the Ottoman version of *fütüvvet*.[26] Neither can it be shown that the Abu al-Najīb al-Suhruwardi, whose essay Naima hoped to put into Ottoman, was concerned with *fütüvvet* (see Section 26). Nevertheless, there is reason to suppose that Ottoman dervish circles in Naima's time were agitating the possibility of revitalizing the older *fütüvvet* idea as a means of strengthening Islam against Christendom as the Abassid caliph al-Nasīr[27] was held to have done in the earlier crisis of attack from the West. This idea may have been in Naima's mind and he may have so worded this passage as to strike a spark in the mind of any initiated reader. All of this, however, must be considered as no more than plausible conjecture. In any event, although the remnants of *fütüvvet* remained alive in the Ottoman Empire into the nineteenth and even the twentieth centuries,[28] it was never revived to be of any consequence, if indeed the attempt to revive it was ever actually made.

43. **Preface One: Section Two**

Section two of the preface consists of two parts: the first being an essay on "The Circumstances Bearing on the Cowardice and Courage of Leaders, both in the Nomadic and Settled Stages; also, The Disastrous Consequences of the Development of Luxury and Ease," and the second an essay on "How Harsh Ministers Cause Despair and so Destroy the Capacity to Wage War" (I, 44–9).[29] The net effect of these two essays is to explain why the Ottoman state had got into such bad shape before Hüseyin Köprülü became grand vezir, and to indict those of his predecessors who had been responsible.

There follow "Several Important Observations: Concerning the Men of the Sword and of the Pen," where Naima points out that both of these classes are necessary to the state, but that there are important differences between them (I, 49–52). It is in the earliest stage and in the two final stages of a state's existence that the men of the sword are indispensable. This explains why, through history, the men of the sword have always been well placed and well off. During a state's middle life, the men of the pen are not only more important, but are also shown more favor and preferment than are the men of the sword.[30] This is due in part to the fact that they are distinctly less dangerous to those who are in power and, in all except the rarest cases, are much more tractable than are the military.

The men of the sword, on the other hand, give their very lives in the service of the faith and the state, but they are at the same time very prone to adopt overweening attitudes and so to become of little practical use. Or else they get out of hand, their support costs the state too much which means that the poor must pay more and more taxes.

From all this it follows that the wise administrator (like Hüseyin Köprülü) must find a middle course, maintaining order with justice and equity for all, but with special privilege for none.

The final portion of section two is a further essay: "Important Observations and Necessary Counsels" (I, 52–8).

When a state is moving from its period of vigorous maturity to its time of decline—that is, in the fourth or fifth of its five stages—the expenditures of the state almost invariably will exceed receipts. Therefore the finances must be closely watched, income and expenditure made to balance, and a surplus accumulated if at all possible. In this time of luxury and display, expensive pomp must be cut down. The administrator must always be on his guard, remembering that at this stage it takes only a few resolute, united men to achieve great results. For, as Mehmed Köprülü himself said, "If only two wise, able men truly join forces, they are able to master the whole world. And it takes only two perfect servants to make the whole world friends of their master, or to make his friends into enemies" (I, 56).

In the time of luxury and decay, no one wants to hold official position. This means that greater care has to be exercised in making appointments, that physical and intellectual training must be encouraged, that attempts must be made to move people by preaching and by example, in time of war and in time of peace, not forgetting how old songs and stories appeal to men.

44. **Preface One: Naima's Conclusions**

With this oblique statement of Hüseyin Köprülü's purposes, Naima arrives at the summation of his Preface One.[31] It is a vigorous statement of faith in the Muslim Ottoman state, buttressed by a concise review of recent Ottoman history. That review stresses the following points:

Kara Mustafa's hostilities with the Hungarians occurred when the Ottoman state was in its fourth stage and therefore suffering from many internal weaknesses. Eventually he failed to take Vienna, and withdrew to Belgrade. Mehmed IV then made a serious error, thanks to bad advice from his councilors: he confiscated Kara Mustafa's property and executed him. This action not only broke the honor of the state—it was the rift in the dam which let in the flood. A series of expensive and futile campaigns ensued. The Venetians, unprovoked, attacked in the Mediterranean, and the evil-souled swine called Moscow occupied the Azak region.

One after another, a succession of grand vezirs tried every expedient. Although they won many short-term successes, in the end they failed. All the while, the Christians' peace proposals were ridiculous; no grand vezir seemed able to make an acceptable peace with them, and conditions steadily grew worse. There was no doubt of the necessity, for the Ottomans, of a breathing spell, a period for domestic rehabilitation to permit them to prepare for war abroad.

In the fifteenth year from the start of the war, the sultan bestowed the grand vezirate upon Hüseyin Köprülü, then commanding at Belgrade, and so solved the problem.

Here follows a touch of immoderate praise of Köprülü—the first immoderate praise in which Naima has indulged in this preface (I, 63). He then resumes his survey: Köprülü's appointment impressed the *Nemçe* (Austrian) emperor who wrote the kings of England and Holland, requesting them to assume the role of mediators. In this move, Venice, Poland, and Moscow joined.[32]

The sultan authorized negotiations, whereupon the grand vezir appointed the *reisülküttab,* Rami Mehmed Pasha, his plenipotentiary. He met the Austrian representatives, and those of Venice, Moscow, and Poland, at Karlowitz.

Here Naima inserts a passage of praises of Rami Pasha.

The treaty was agreed upon. İbrahim Pasha went on embassy to Austria, and ambassadors were exchanged by all parties. Here Naima brings the preface to an end with the note that, "All of these events will be given in detail under the proper year in the history which follows, God Willing!"

45. **Summary of Preface One**

Leaving aside the section on history which will be discussed in Section 60, we may now evaluate Naima's preface for Köprülü, and what that preface reveals of Naima himself.

It is a skillful composition: Köprülü should have felt that Naima deserved reward. The blending of political propaganda into the preface form is masterful. There is a general tone of fearlessness and an absence of the calculating and the servile which will encourage all but the most skeptical to believe that Naima was actually convinced of the truth and right of what he wrote.

He loses no chance to appeal to his readers. The style—only a relatively "high style" apart from the section from Nabi, but nevertheless distinctly higher than Naima's normal style in the history proper—was the style popular among educated Ottomans of the time, and may represent some concession on Naima's part with a view to convincing the reader.[33] The approach is that which would appeal to the most bigoted of Köprülü's opponents and which would be most difficult for them to refute. The works quoted—Nabi, Kâtip Çelebi, Âli, and Kınalızade's *Ahlak-ı Alâî*—are without exception among the most esteemed works of Ottoman literature.

The preface was as well designed to please its patron as it was to present that patron's case to his critics. Certainly the view of history that it sets forth, although by no means original with Naima, is a view that the modern world would not care to dismiss. Knowledge that such ideas were still living issues in the Ottoman Empire of the early eighteenth century is a useful corrective against the tendency to dismiss that empire as simply another decadent oriental state.

This preface is a concrete indication that the Ottomans' major difficulty was not that they lacked ideas or conviction or even idealism; rather it was that the Ottomans as leaders of the Muslim world and Muslim civilization, had grown to be so self-contained, so sure that they themselves embodied the good and the true, that they failed to pay the indispensable minimum of attention to the "heathen." Naima apparently knows practically nothing of contemporary Europe, and very little of the Europe of the past. He is a liberal in Ottoman terms, open minded and inquisitive within the framework of the Ottoman's Muslim civilization. Yet he sees nothing incongruous in comparing eighteenth-century Europe—the Europe of Prince Eugene, Marlborough, and Louis XIV—with the Europe of the Crusaders. Each had many *Nemçe,* and they had an emperor! Certainly Naima was well educated, in terms of his own world. It is equally certain that that education did not equip the individual to defend his world against the new challenges that a new Europe was already pressing home.[34]

46. **Preface Two: Structure**

Naima's Preface Two, the unfinished preface written in 1703–04 for Grand Vezir Moralı Hasan, is somewhat less coherent and less elaborate than Preface One (VI, App.). Its structure is as follows:

(P. 2 Introductory note by the publisher, İbrahim Müteferrika.)

I. Introduction (pp. 2–4).
   - A. Circumstances of writing (pp. 2–4).
   - B. Prayer (p. 4).

II. The Preface proper (pp. 4–58).
   - A. Dedication: to Sultan Ahmed III and Grand Vezir Moralı Hasan Pasha (pp. 4–5).
   - B. On Mufti Feyzullah (pp. 5–19).
     1. His background and his conduct (pp. 5–7).
     2. An objection and answer: concerning family dynasties among the ulema and the role of the ulema in the affairs of state (pp. 7–10).
     3. An objection and answer: the ulema and the ministers should be mutually complementary, each checking and balancing the other. The role of the vezir (pp. 10–13).

4. Anecdote: a dispute between Naima and a partisan of Feyzullah, before the Edirne Incident (pp. 13–18).
5. Excursus: on the ulema in politics (pp. 18–19).

C. Narrative of the Edirne Incident (pp. 19–52).
1. Narrative (pp. 19–26).
2. The sultan's courage, etc. (pp. 26–31).
3. Narrative concluded (pp. 31–36).
4. Hasan Pasha's courage (pp. 36–43).
5. Noble moral (pp. 43–52).

D. Conclusion (pp. 52–58).

Two parts of this preface have been presented in Section 26.

47. **Preface Two: Narrative and Background**

Naima opens the preface proper by avowing that he is here presenting an abridged, condensed version of the "Edirne Incident" in order to set forth the virtues of Ahmed III and of Moralı Hasan.

To do this, he must first recount the story of the Mufti Feyzullah Efendi whose behavior had been the principal cause of the Edirne Incident.

Feyzullah's foolishness, his pomp and vanity, his nepotism, his interference in matters where no mufti had ever before interfered, and his evident resolution to make himself, as mufti (and not as grand vezir), the chief administrative official of the state; all these are presented and condemned.

Naima then shows that this specific condemnation of Feyzullah is not to be construed as a blanket criticism of the entire ulema body. There is nothing wrong in family dynasties in the ulema, families of which several members may successively rise to become mufti. Examples are the famous Sadeddin family and the Kara Çelebizade family (see Section 69). But these families, unlike that of Feyzullah, lived frugally. Although keenly interested in the appointments made within the ulema corps, they did not mix into other spheres of politics and of appointments, nor did they indulge in polemic.

Naima then develops the point that the proper role of the ulema in the state is that of overseers and preceptors. By nature, the grand vezir's office is under the sultan, the seat of the final temporal authority in the state; the nonpolitical ulema, headed by the mufti, should act as spiritual and moral checks and balances to the temporal power, but they should not themselves wield temporal power as Feyzullah Efendi, in contravention of the "natural order," had attempted to do.

Naima then recounts, to his own credit, an argument that he had had with a supporter of Feyzullah's pretensions at the time when the mufti was at the height of his power. Naima, although it meant that he had to be rude, as a historian and a scribe held to the convictions expressed above, and manfully argued back to his haughty ulema opponent.

This section concludes with an excursus to the effect that politics inevitably entails intrigue and conniving, and that this is less seemly and more shameful for the ulema than for any other class of men.

There follows Naima's narrative of the Edirne Incident or revolt of 1703, the revolt that brought Sultan Ahmed III to the throne. This narrative is frankly designed to show the sultan and his brother-in-law and grand vezir, Moralı Hasan, in the best possible light. Thus it is partisan history and so, alone among what we have of Naima's writings, deserves to be called "official historian's" history in the sense that it is an out-and-out apology for the actions of the contemporary sultan and grand vezir. This is not, of course, to claim that Naima's account of the revolt is falsified. Moralı Hasan Pasha evidently had been at least sympathetic to the forces that, Hüseyin Köprülü and, later, Rami Mehmed Pasha had represented, and had opposed their opponents, particularly Feyzullah Efendi and his adherents. It may be that the same assertions would also hold to a degree for Ahmed III himself. So for Naima to write as their partisan did not mean that he adopted new views on the spur of the moment in an attempt to retain his official position. Preface Two is full of flattery, but it scarcely descends to sycophancy. Its underlying ideas are those which one presumes Naima would have harbored in any case.

Naima first interrupts his narrative of the revolt to insert a section in praise of Ahmed III's course (VI, App. 19–26). Ahmed had early warned Mustafa II, his predecessor who was destined to be dethroned by the revolt, against giving the mufti that prominence and power that Mustafa II nevertheless continued to lavish on him. Then when trouble came, Ahmed III took active measures to defend himself, measures admirable as an example of resolute self-defense. Thirdly, during the revolt Ahmed III did not hesitate when confronted with the threats of the greedy, uncurbed troops, but bravely faced them down. Finally, he had borne himself bravely and maturely throughout, especially in the way in which he managed the clever wording of the amnesty, which ended the revolt: "You may be sure that, so long as on your part there is no stand or activity contrary to the *şerıat* or the *kanun* or harmful to the faith and the state, on my part there will appear no reproach or retaliation" (VI, App. 30). In addition, once he had become sultan, Ahmed III instituted a laudable program of personal economies.

Returning to the narrative, Naima carries it forward to the appointment of Moralı Hasan as grand vezir, and then interrupts his story again, this time to insert a section in praise of Hasan (VI, App. 31–6). Hasan's principal services, as Naima sees them, were first, that he restrained Mustafa II from a course that would have inflamed the Edirne Incident into open civil war. Secondly, by staying at his post in Edirne, Hasan Pasha through his diplomacy was able to save the city. Thirdly, when he became grand vezir, Hasan Pasha executed none of his opponents but, instead, magnanimously recalled the ulema who had been exiled and even treated Feyzullah Efendi's own family with kindness and generosity.

In the grand vezirate, Moralı Hasan Pasha has proven to be a hard-working man, personally very frugal, giving his attention to the problem of rearming the state. He does not participate in or approve of bribery, and he is extremely charitable to the Muslims.

48. **Preface Two: Naima's Conclusions**

In an elegant Excursus (VI, App. 43–52), Naima reviews the causes of the Edirne Incident, the earthly causes and the astrological causes, and only then is ready to present his "Conclusion of Conclusions," the most mature political wisdom he can offer:

From Naima, VI, Appendix, 52–4
Conclusion of Conclusions

This eternity-joined Ottoman state is the benefactor of each and every Muslim. The peace of mind and the security of Muhammad's people are dependent upon this sublime state. Therefore it is necessary and incumbent that all who are able should serve this state with their property and with their bodies. Also, every man should set forth all the helpful facts which he knows, whether they be insights that he has attained or things that he has heard: for a man thus to show himself a well-wisher of the state must not be counted as a breach of propriety. The saying goes: "Take that which is pure: spurn that which troubles." It should be acted upon; wise counsel should be accepted; words that do not comport with the time in which we live should be abandoned. None of these things will prove to be useless. And the well-wisher [of the state] who does set forth his advice ought not to encounter criticism and objections.

For these reasons, I [Naima], humble and full of faults, have set forth such ideas as my poor intellect has been able to grasp: it is hoped that this prideful presumption will be condoned.

At the present time—Praise be to God!—the effort and exertions that our highly active master of the state and lord [Ahmed III] is putting forth to organize state affairs are truly the finest, and his labors for successful administration are so excellent that never in recent times could it have been said that the vital concerns of the state were so well looked after or that every matter was being undertaken with a comparable regard for the natural requirements of the case.

May God, the great and high, enable him to achieve order and organization, and to put an end to the things that harm the finances.

There are five principles that are the most important and necessary of all for the affairs of the sublime state, the most difficult and the most telling of all for solving the difficulties of the sultanate. It is these principles that, in every century, humble and confound great kings and lofty vezirs. It is virtually certain that in a state that is properly conducted according to these five articles, dissension and weakening will not thenceforth appear.

First: *An attempt should be made subtly to get expenses and income to balance, perhaps through some means of reducing expenditures. But the people should not be irritated by having their names struck off the state payrolls; no individual should be given cause to complain because his allowances have been reduced or his pay cut; nor should this make necessary any emergency levies or the levying of any new taxes.*

Second: *A way should be found through some philosophical stratagem to get rid of the practice of postponed payment; that burdensome curse should be removed from the imperial treasury. But this should be done in such a way that no man will be moved to charge injustice, complaining that "The government withholds money due me."*

Third: *The various military organizations should be put into shape through just means to the end that the different corps will be at full strength. This should be done not only to enable them to withstand the enemy in time of need, but also to prevent the* taslakçı[35] *class in the provinces from wronging the government,* zaimler, *and* evkaf *by concealing what is right; and also to make sure that the military will not be able to disobey or to do wrong in the capital or anywhere else in the state but will be as tractable to authority as are bond slaves.*

Fourth: *The outlying provinces and the whole state should be exploited and administered so that the peasants will have security and the lands of Islam will be prosperous, and so that the government will get full revenue, and the governors and commanders will receive their profits and thus can maintain their local households at full strength and fully equipped.*

Fifth: *Let it be beguilingly and subtly arranged that the padishah of Islam, when he is informally in the company of those notables who are his intimates, shall be as cheerful as is reasonably possible. Thus affection for him and dread of him will together be insinuated into the hearts of the people so that in the future, both in the capital and in the provinces, the people will not only not rebel or band together, but also so that eventually wrongdoing of this sort will not even occur to their minds as a possibility, for they will wholeheartedly obey and submit to the sultan and the ministers of the state.*

If, with divine aid, the application of these principles be easily attained, there would remain no further difficulty. It would be perfectly easy to answer the foes of the faith and the state and to deal with every matter in the desired way.

Naima notes that some may object that these five principles are impossible to put into practice, that they are mutually contradictory and that, in any event, they constitute a long-term program and so would not meet the present emergency (VI, App. 54). His answer to this is the assertion that the essay by Suhrawardi, if translated and put into the hands of the sultan and grand vezir, would show that this program is perfectly feasible. This section has been presented in Section 26.

49. **Summary of Preface Two**

Although less striking than Preface One, Preface Two—even in its incomplete form—is no less skillful a composition. Its principal value lies in the clarity with which it shows that, in the upshot, the Edirne revolt had changed almost nothing. The same emergency persisted. The same dissensions racked the state as had been the case under Hüseyin Köprülü and Rami Mehmed. Naima's tone is that of the courtier, but of a courtier who does not hesitate to speak his mind, contributing for the use of the ruler all the insights he himself has attained and all the useful points that he has heard. Thus this preface is less derivative than any other of Naima's extant writings.

50. **Nasihat**

Wholly a child of his own times, Naima of course believed unquestioningly in personal government, in the direct rule of the sultan or (failing a strong sultan) of the grand vezir under the ultimate sanction of the Muslim faith. His own "helpful points"—the insights he has attained and the things he has learned from others—are presented as the *raison d'être* of his history. In this sense, the chronicle is simply the vehicle that carries the "helpful points." It is not primarily designed to carry them to the commonality but rather to the elite—to the rulers and the class from which the rulers and their advisers come. Thus Naima is dealing in a sort of *nasihat* literature, the literature of "Good Counsels for Rulers."[36] The "good counsels" upon which he lays the most stress will now occupy us. He does not present them in a logical scheme, not even in his relatively well-organized preface, and they do not constitute a "system." They are no more than what Naima says they are: practical, specific morals drawn from history and intended for the ear of the rulers who, he knows, must save the Ottoman state if it is to be saved at all. For the most part, they are concerned with what the individual ruler—Hüseyin Köprülü, Sultan Ahmed III, Moralı Hasan—should or should not do. To a lesser degree Naima's good counsels refer to the government machine, to the organized groups and factions in the state, but here again he is primarily concerned with how a ruler can best overhaul the machine and how to operate it once it has been overhauled.

To the unsympathetically critical modern reader, parochial in terms of his own Western European civilization, Naima's insights may seem to be no more than platitudes. To the reader more familiar with Ottoman, and indeed with all Oriental literature, it will seem that Naima did speak much wisdom and that he indulged in surprisingly plain speaking for his time and place, and that Naima's recommendations were by no means merely platitudinous, however diffuse their form and however ineffectual most of them proved to be.

51. On Leadership

Naima frequently alludes to the necessity for effective leadership, leadership of skill and courage, in the military and civil establishments alike. The requirements of good leadership are well illustrated by two passages concerning a proverbial Ottoman military leader, Tiryaki Hasan Pasha, the defender of Kanice, and by a third passage describing the bravery of Hafız Pasha, an unfortunate grand vezir under Murad IV.

The first passage on Tiryaki Hasan Pasha is entitled "*Nasihat*" (I, 273). It is appended to a section of narrative, "The Wise Measures Taken by the Vezir Hasan Pasha," which had emphasized the success Tiryaki Hasan gained in successfully defending Kanice fortress during the siege of the summer of 1601. Hasan Pasha showed particular cleverness in arousing the old frontier ghazi spirit among his men and also in his use of stratagems.

Naima adds:

From Naima, I, 273

In major frontier undertakings of this sort, what one must have is an intelligent man to lead the troops, a man as skillful and resourceful as was this [Hasan Pasha], a man who will pay no attention to every outcry that is raised but who instead is strong-hearted. If that be the case, the troops serving under him will take confidence from his actions. They will rely upon what he says. Their courage will be reinforced by his efforts to strengthen it. Beyond this, their hearts will be united and their counsels at one and, in consequence, results will be obtained. In such times of stress, patience and resolution are indispensable [in the commander]. There is a saying [in Arabic], "A pinch of guile is a greater help than a tribe." In the proper use of surprises and strategems there is indeed a vast amount of benefit.

After describing Tiryaki Hasan Pasha's ultimate victory over Archduke Ferdinand at Kanice, Naima adds a further note—a "Word of Admonition" (I, 282–6). He notes that the Ottoman troops who by night occupied the position from which the Archduke had fled did not at once plunder his tents. Instead, since they were sure that their commander would divide the booty fairly, they waited till morning. This not only illustrates the rectitude of the troops and the completeness of their obedience to Hasan Pasha. It also shows how uncorrupted Hasan Pasha was, how free of greed, what a fine character he had. And "in every case where the troops are thus obedient and the commander thus noble, God has ever granted victory" (I, 286).

Above all, it is courage and pride, even unreasonable courage and pride, that maintain morale. In the account of the reign of the young Sultan Murad IV, in 1631 shortly before that sultan shook off his advisers and began to rule in fact as well as in name, Naima's sources relate the history of a rising that caused the dismissal and finally the death of Grand Vezir Hafız Pasha (II, 84 seq.) One particular passage in this long narrative portrays the unfortunate grand vezir's last formal procession to the divan meeting. As he was making his way through the troubled city he encountered a messenger whom Bayram Pasha, one of the vezirs, had just sent out to warn the grand vezir that he should not attend the divan that day but instead should immediately go into hiding.

This messenger came up to Hafız Pasha and delivered Bayram Pasha's warning. "The grand vezir laughed and answered him, 'Go back and greet your master for me! In my dreams I have foreseen the inexorable decree which will be made manifest [his death]—but death does not oppress me!' " (II, 86).

Here Naima is stirred to interrupt his source's narrative. He says, "[Hafız Pasha] meant that when a grandee, truly 'disposer of the people's affairs,' was approaching the imperial palace in full pomp, then to ask the holder of that office to do nothing—even to go back to his own residence without having himself surrendered custody of the seal to his master—this was such wrongful shame that death itself was easier" (II, 86).

52. **On Executions**

Courageous and proud loyalty could easily cost an honest Ottoman leader his life, for capital punishment of officials, especially of grand vezirs, had become a true plague in the system. When Naima was writing, this practice was—for the time being—in relative abeyance, but the course of his chronicle gave him ample opportunity to examine it. He makes two observations of interest, the first critical of the practice, the second admitting that an opponent's death is often opportune although it should not be sought.

Soon after becoming grand vezir, Mehmed Köprülü had deposed the *vali* (governor) of Egypt, one Kara Mustafa Pasha.[37] Mustafa Pasha returned to Istanbul overland. The grand vezir attempted but failed to arrest him as he was passing through Syria. Mustafa Pasha then succeeded in fleeing incognito to the capital, giving rise to his nickname, Firari (the Fugitive). He lived in Istanbul in hiding for some years until pardoned by Fazıl Ahmed Köprülü.[38]

An otherwise unimportant passage in Naima's account, "The affair of Firari Kara Mustafa Pasha," includes a supplement of interest, based in part on Naima's personal knowledge of Aleppo traditions (VI, 273–6). One of the officials whom Mehmed Köprülü had instructed to apprehend Mustafa Pasha had been Abaza Hasan

Pasha, governor of Aleppo. The accepted story is that Abaza Hasan did try to arrest the ex-governor, but failed.

Naima, however, says:

From Naima, VI, 275–6

It has been heard from certain of the well-informed leading men of Aleppo that Abaza Hasan Pasha did set out from Aleppo to catch Mustafa Pasha, as he had been ordered to do. But since he himself did not feel sure of the grand vezir, he reflected, "Why should a man soil his honor with the crime of killing a well-reputed vezir?" Accordingly, he sent ahead word [to Mustafa Pasha] saying, "You take secretly to flight." If this really is the way in which Mustafa Pasha's flight took place, then it was indeed occasioned by advance information. This story does seem reasonable. Abaza Hasan Pasha's subsequent actions would confirm it.

It has frequently happened that vezirs and special messengers when under orders to slay a reputable vezir have refused to do so, either because they feared God's vengeance, or else because they were not willing to have a hand in such hateful work. They delicately forewarn the intended victim, pretending that they themselves are ignorant of the whole affair. So they cause the man to flee and to get to safety. We have even observed cases in which the trusted servant of one or another vezir supposedly "betrays" his master. He sends a warning, apparently treating a hated foe as a friend, and so enables the "foe" to flee. But there is no reason to doubt that the servant in fact sent the warning with his master's secret approval. All this will be related in its proper place.

To do this thing [to enable the condemned man to flee] is in itself laudable. In this particular case Kara Mustafa Pasha secretly reached Istanbul, lived there for a number of years in hiding, and eventually his sons were pardoned in the time of Fazıl Ahmed Pasha, as will be related in due course.

Even Mehmed Köprülü was sometimes spared the necessity of executing an opponent when the man chanced to die from natural causes. Such an incident gives Naima an opening to observe that it is indeed opportune to have one's opponents removed. The man in question was an opponent of Köprülü's, the janissary leader Kara Hasanzade Hüseyin Agha who died in the first year of Köprülü's grand vezirate. Naima gives at length Kara Çelebizade Abdülâziz Efendi's extremely hostile account of the agha, then adds a word of restraint (VI, 295–9). Hüseyin Agha should not really be held to deserve all the abuse that has been heaped upon him. He very likely had some share in the removal of Abdülâziz from the office of mufti; Abdülâziz here—"thanks to his own nature"—is getting his revenge by slandering the agha. As a matter of fact, Hüseyin Agha had rendered several signal services to the state. On the other hand, his efforts to undermine Mehmed Köprülü were ill-advised, and his death, from Köprülü's point of view, was certainly opportune for it allowed the grand vezir at last to get a firm grip on the janissary corps.

53. **On a Strong Ruler**

To Naima, the greatest good for the state is a strong sultan. This is strikingly illustrated by his appraisal of Sultan Murad IV.

From Naima, III, 170–72 [Year 1043/began July 8, 1633]

[*Recounting Sultan Murad IV's strenuous and well-known efforts to close all coffee-houses and forbid the use of tobacco, Naima inserts the following personal opinion and anecdote.*] *The humble one* [*Naima*] *may state that the fact that the late Sultan Murad* [*IV*] *was so severe, and that he threatened to patrol the streets and to put men to death as part of his abolition of coffee-houses and of smoking, was not merely a wanton prohibition or simply arbitrariness. Rather, it is plain that this was a pretext for the purpose of controlling the riffraff and for frightening the common people in the interests of the state. Now experienced, responsible men who themselves investigate the behind-the-scenes facts concerning the rebels* [*of Sultan Murad IV's day*] *and who realize the difficulties and troubles which that proud padishah experienced from these riffraff—all matters which have been fully set forth above—take into consideration the wholly good intention and the general benefit which were present underneath this severity and rigor.*[39] *They perceive that at that time it was absolutely indispensable to terrify the general populace with the well-tempered sword if those who had forsaken the path of obedience and who were opposing the imperial will were to be brought back to the right way and made of use* [*to the state*].

At that time coffee and tobacco were neither more nor less than a pretext for assembling; a crowd of good-for-nothings was forever meeting in coffee-houses or barber shops or in the houses of certain men—houses which were places on the order of club-houses—where they would spend their time criticizing and disparaging the great and the authorities, waste their breath discussing imperial interests connected with affairs of state, dismissals and appointments, fallings out and reconciliations, and so they would gossip and lie.

Because he himself knew this to be the case, [*the sultan*] *prohibited* [*coffee and tobacco*]. *He himself would go through the city, patrol it day and night, arrest and put to death those riffraff and rebels and tobacco-parties whom he found by day, and make the carefree night-owls drink the cup of death. The fear of the padishah's sword so pervaded humble and great that no man could say a word about the padishah, not even in his own home. So, following the saying, "The walls have ears," they let example be the wise man's conscience.*

In fact His Excellency Sivasizade told me that the late padishah [*Murad IV*] *much of the time went about in disguise, spying out what the men of the time were up to.*[40] *On one occasion the Şeyh Efendi* (*Sivasizade*) *and certain holy confreres had gone* [*on a picnic*] *to the Mirahor kiosk at Kağıthane.*[41] *While they were amusing themselves there with learned intercourse, intellectual companionship, and Sufi discussion, His Majesty Sultan Murad* Han *approached unobserved in his boat. He had it pulled in to the shore and sent a man to bring him the books of the men present there, and also of the things which they had with them at their gathering. As he was looking these over, a copy of Yahya Efendi's* Divan *caught his eye and he exclaimed, "Why! This is my efendi's* Divan.*" After he had inspected the other books as well, he said, "I have nothing to say against, and I do not interfere with ulema who take their books and go on a picnic, or against dervishes who go with their rosaries and prayer-rugs and shawls, or yet against scribes with their pen-cases and pens and their writing materials. Let these men at once go back to their own pleasures!" And he departed. The aforesaid Aziz* [*Sivasizade*] *received high distinction in the reign of the late padishah* [*Murad IV*], *was frequently in conversation and companionship with him, and went to His Royal Majesty confidentially on a number of matters. It will be good if, God exalted willing, the particulars be heard from his own noble tongue and inserted into this history.*

In this fashion the late padishah took even this degree of pains in administering the state.

54. **On Influencing Sultans**

In the case of a less than strong sultan, the question of influencing the sultan becomes vital. Such influence should be exerted in the best interests of the state and not selfishly. The sultan himself, moreover, should be on his guard against men who seek to influence him for selfish ends.

These points are illustrated by Naima's comments upon two events, one from the time of İbrahim, the other from the reign of his older brother and predecessor, Murad IV.

Among the events of 1052 (began April 1, 1642) Naima reproduces an account given by Vecihi of how Sultan İbrahim, executed Silihdar Mustafa who had been Murad IV's favorite but was the foe of the grand vezir, Kemankeş Kara Mustafa Pasha (IV, 11–12). Vecihi implies that the silihdar's fate was well deserved. He had diverted to his own pocket the Cyprus revenue whose proper use was to pay the troops. With this assertion of Vecihi's, Naima's predecessor compiler, Şarih al-Manarzade, has disagreed (IV, 12–13). Their conflicting statements afford Naima an opportunity to state his own views on how affairs should have been conducted and also—by implication—on how they should be conducted now and henceforth.

From Naima, IV, 13–14

This humble one would state that the padishah's intimates, especially those who have found advancement and glory in the title of vezir, have always been men of influence in the Sublime State. They have always had favors and gifts from the padishah. They have always intruded into the conduct of affairs, obtaining appointments for various clever men. They have always had their own protégés. They have always profited from the revenue of the Sublime State in one or another way.

Although these practices have not always had laudable results, they are nonetheless established usages for all that. Granted that to take anything from the Sublime State is detestable, the fact remains that the correct punishment for this is confiscation of property and forced restitution.

For the followers and supporters of grand vezirs and noble officials to do their utmost in order to get their masters close to the seat of power is a natural if regrettable thing. It stems from the love of position and the desire for appointments. But the punishment for this is to admonish them through banishment with subsequent forgiveness, or else through confiscation of property.

Form this it follows that there is no absolute excuse for the execution of the aforesaid [*Silihdar Mustafa*]*. On the other hand, because he esteemed power and took pride in novelty the Silihdar Pasha had come to vaunt himself in the padishah's favor. He had caused the unjust execution of Tabanıbüyük Mehmed Pasha and of several other individuals—with no thought for the consequences—as has been related in the appropriate places. Since the nature of being is based upon rewards and punishments, there is no doubt that he deserved punishment for his malpractices and that what was manifested was divine revenge.*

The risk of the sultan's not guarding himself against bad influences is brought out in a comment that Naima prefaces to his transcription of a well-known poetical exchange—the ghazels of Hafız Pasha and Murad IV. Hafız Pasha had failed to retake Baghdad from the Persians. He wrote a military communiqué in verse to which the sultan replied in kind.[42] The sultan's verse is, to Naima, a prime example of unjustified ingratitude. Naima adds another "Note of Caution." Hafız Pasha should not be blamed for his failure; he should be praised for doing as well as he did. He had almost no funds. His supplies were cut off. His men's morale was destroyed. He was continually troubled by outlaws. Despite all this he held out, prolonged the siege, eventually retired with honor, and distinctly deserved the sultan's gratitude. But various detractors had meantime got the sultan's ear. They turned him against Hafız Pasha who, they claimed, was giving the untenanted feudal holdings to his own favorites. Hafız was accused of having abandoned his army on various pretexts, of being personally responsible for the failure to take Baghdad, and the like. Thus he unjustly came to suffer the sultan's ingratitude.

55. **For Grand Vezirs**

Noteworthy sections in which Naima addresses advice directly to politicians, especially to grand vezirs, reiterate the points that a man's ultimate strength is his friends, that no one can hope to please everybody, but that success is contingent on early winning and always retaining enough true supporters to defend one's fortunes.

In the year 1058 (began January 27, 1648) Naima relates the story of Grand Vezir Hezarpare Ahmed Pasha's deposition and violent death (IV, 306 seq.). Into this account Naima's predecessor, Şarih al-Manarzade, had inserted the observation that this grand vezir would have done well not to have fled from his palace when trouble developed, but to have barricaded himself there. Had he done so, he might have saved his life. Then he would have been able to relinquish the grand vezirate in return for a provincial governorship, perhaps at Buda.

Naima objects:

From Naima, IV, 310–11

The humble one [Naima] would state that this is not excluded but that if it had been possible to prepare oneself against the mob, the padishah would have done so. Certainly this fortification of his palace could not have been equal to the defensive possibilities of the imperial palace.

When the men of the ocaks *and the ulema as well are one's enemies to the death, it is scarcely conceivable that one can fortify and defend oneself within the city of Istanbul. The fate of Siyavuş Pasha who recently attempted this will be related in its proper place.*

One's only real defense is one's friends. However, are those bastard "supporters" of pashas—those "supporters" who plunder their pashas' palaces while the fate of their pashas is still uncertain—are they working in the interests of their masters? But hold! had he [Ahmed Pasha] actually "gone forth" with a provincial governorship, there still would have been no assurance that he could save himself. Thus this assertion [by Şarih al-Manarzade] is beside the point.

What [Ahmed Pasha] should have done, logically, was immediately and at the time for action to find a loyal friend of proven faith and sincerity.

Then—taking with him plenty of gold—he should have hidden himself properly, with that friend's knowledge. Later on, when times had changed and affairs had taken on another complexion, he could have acted through that friend and so easily have reappeared. But he had failed to prepare for this ahead of time, and he failed to distinguish loyal men from flatterers.

It is related on the authority of Telhisi Abdi that Ahmed Pasha was a self-indulgent, corpulent man. That night, when the troops were on the prowl everywhere and drunk on arak, *Abdi said [to him] with a bitter sigh, "Oh, Efendim, you have not found any especial friend or loyal helper against this day. Alas!"*

When he said this, the pasha sighed regretfully and replied, "Ah, my boy, we did not know that this was the way things were going to turn out!"

Then Halil, the slave who was attending him and who appears to have been a sensible lad, said, "Oh, Efendim, this is the result of all the things you have done and of the things you have not done since the beginning of your vezirate. It has been perfectly plain that this was how it would turn out. But you have been blinded by power and have not yourself been on your guard to take any precautions. Neither were your well-wishers, although they saw your pride and your arrogance, able to arouse you. Now may God save you speedily."

The essence of the matter is this: Ahmed Pasha was deceived by his own clever wit, his foresight, and his intelligence. He had come to mock and laugh at those who gave him good advice. If he was on terms of friendly intimacy with a man, he strove to turn this fact to worldly gain. It was his consistent policy to use his friends for some short-term advantage, some everyday concern. It never entered his head to make a friend who would be a blessing when evil times should come.

Not even the best grand vezir can please everyone. Partisanship will prove too strong for him. This is well illustrated in the account of another grand vezir's dismissal and execution, that of Sufi Mehmed Pasha (IV, 406). Naima summarizes the different judgments which earlier historians have passed on Sufi Mehmed Pasha. Kâtip Çelebi and Mehmed Pasha criticize him severely. Kara Çelebizade praises him. Şarih al-Manarzade is critical (IV, 410–11). To Naima it appears that there should be a middle road.

From Naima, IV, 410–11

It is out of the question for all the characteristics and actions of grand vezirs and other dignitaries in the government to be praiseworthy, or for everything they do in directing and financing state affairs to please people. It makes no difference in how many praiseworthy, laudable matters a man succeeds, still he is bound also to do other things which will cause dissatisfaction, whether he wish it or not.

Ever since the time of the Prophet and the period of the orthodox caliphate, it has been extremely rare for pure justice and unmixed equity to prevail, or for every single matter to be dealt with exactly as it ought to be. Especially when the state is weak, cliques appear and partisans predominate. This means that to treat every interest as it deserves is almost inconceivable.

Even if they all are treated in what is—according to the exigencies of that time—the best possible way, it still is not possible to free one's collar from the opponent's stab and from the hubbub of the jealous.

Those who have enjoyed favor and honor from a vezir, who have had some part in affairs and some share of power during his term of office, hold that he was an excellent man. They praise and honor him. They describe his every praiseworthy phase. And, since they seek to gain him good prayers until eternity, they write at length.

But those who had no share of power [under the vezir] and were left out—and who, it may be, are also overweening, malicious men—ever keep before themselves the bad phases. In order to set forth his failures and disgrace, they take to criticizing and damning him. God knows the truth.

56. **On Factions**

Handling the various corps and political factions of the empire was one of an Ottoman statesman's major concerns.

Naima's account of the murder of Kösem, the Queen Mother, leads him to reflect upon this problem (IV, 114). He begins by registering the difference of opinion about Kösem; some hold that she was a generous, almsgiving woman. Others call her greedy and grasping, and this is the opinion that Şarih al-Manarzade has adopted. Naima takes another approach:

From Naima, V, 115–16

Even if the Old Valide had given up her amassing of wealth, her generosity and her philanthropy, and even if she had not interfered in any affair, still—at a time when the men who enjoyed the state's profits and the government revenues were overweening, covetous aghas of this sort—what is there to show that they would have applied the revenues to their proper objects? Indeed, it was absolutely certain that the suppression and extermination of the aghas and the liquidation of their temeritous association would be contingent upon some such infamous happening. Thus there is no question but that what transpired was due to divine wisdom, and that the respected valide, philanthropic and regal as she was, was martyred for the sake of those unjust oppressions.

There is no power and no strength except those of God the high and great! Abu Bakr the True—May God be pleased with him—said: "Remember the loss of the Prophet which spread among you a great blow for you all!" In accord with this wise saying, those who consider the orthodox caliphs and especially how Hasan and Hüseyin, who saw the light of the seal of the prophets, were—thanks to various hidden decrees and divine secrets—martyred at a time of religious dissension, those who with true reflection perceive the secret of how many great sultans and famous men have been betrayed and killed, thanks to rebellions which arose for the purpose of getting transitory power or attaining human goals—such men will not be troubled or grieved by worrisome happenings of this sort.

This, also, is not concealed from the heart of the truth-seeker: in the Sublime State, in every period, the influence of speech and free action has fallen to the share of one group [or another]. *And then until the time when, divine will permitting, influence and control pass from that corps to another corps, it is no more than natural for each group to vaunt itself foolishly while it has the royal favor and to rejoice in receiving profits to its heart's content. But one must add at least this much: those who attain to glory and favor through especial fortune of this sort must, no matter who they are, behave with good sense, and must not fail to observe the limits which the rights of God and of the people constitute. Those who do this have ever been wont to have a long term of power with real success, being strengthened by divine help against the stratagems of the world. But those who take the way of excess and remissness, never understand, in any matter, what the right of justice is—and it is the cornerstone of the order of the being of existence. Or else they fail to observe it. There is no doubt that the scale of conformity [justice] does weigh down, and that people have ever fallen in a short time from the station of honor.*

In an earlier passage Naima has already made the point that the Old Valide should not be accused of blind partisanship for the janissary aghas. Şarih al-Manarzade, Kâtip Çelebi, and Kara Çelebizade are unanimously agreed in their account of the dismissal of Melek Ahmed Pasha from the grand vezirate and the subsequent appointment of Siyavuş Pasha (V, 102–3). Naima, however, has a different and, he feels, more reliable version:

From Naima, V, 103

Conversing with Maanoğlu about events of this time I have heard the following: The Old Valide was in truth the protector and supporter of the aghas. On the day alluded to, however, a certain wise man had stated, "If the ocak *aghas are to be put down in response to the people's having assembled and demanded it, then hereafter whenever the dregs of the city start something, it will be difficult to get them under control. Regardless of any other thing, it is vital to break up this demonstration."*

It was as a result of this (and not because of her partisanship for the aghas) that Her Majesty the valide commanded for them to be dispersed.

57. **The Sipahi**s

Naima gives special attention to one of the organized corps of the state, the *sipahi*s, by appending a moral concerning them to his account of their revolt against Grand Vezir Sufi Mehmed Pasha in 1058 (began January 15, 1649).

From Naima, IV, 351

The cause of this organization's having somehow gotten out of control is this. Every military organization should have several ranks of officers. For them—high and low—to be controlled, for the whole of them ultimately to be disciplined and organized under a commander-in-chief, is an important principle. It is important both as a usage of the civil government and also of the military organization. For example, in the janissaries each oda *[room] has its veterans who are, so to speak, officers over the other men. Above them are the cooks; above these are the room heads and soupmakers. The superior officer of the room heads and soupmakers is the steward, and over him is the superior of them all, the agha.*

In the olden days the sipahis *were also formed on this principle. However many troops there were, each troop had its troop head, comparable to the janissary room head. He knew and controlled the men in his troop. Today he cannot be distinguished from the other men.*

As time went on the authority of these men was taken from them and concentrated solely in the [sipahi] agha, steward and the çavuslar. *It is because fifteen officers, all of whom are of but one or two ranks, cannot control five or ten thousand men that this organization's veterans and rookies, men of rank and men in the ranks, cannot be distinguished one from the other. They [the* sipahis*] have become appendages of the other organization in name and in commanders and leaders.*

58. **Kalem Reforms**

Detailed suggestions for reform in the Ottoman government are introduced at only one place in Naima's chronicle. They concern the *kalem* and are specifically restricted to it alone.

One of the obituary notices appended to the account of the events in 1068 (began October 9, 1657) is that of the *defterdar* Sarı Ali Efendi (VI, 307). Here Naima first reproduces Kara Çelebizade's remarks on Sarı Ali, then adds a word of remonstrance against Kara Çelebizade's extreme views. Naima identifies this Sarı Ali Efendi as the father of a man well known in his own time, the recent defterdar bey efendi who had become vezir—and subsequently died—during the reign of Süleyman II. Sarı Ali, the father, had in reality been an excellent official, and during the grand vezirate of Mehmed Köprülü had corrected many financial abuses and accomplished important reforms. These very reforms were what had won for him the general unpopularity which Kara Çelebizade's account reflects.

Mention of this leads Naima to introduce a series of observations on the question of how to reform the financial administration. His principal point is a warning against the practice of *kat-ı erzak,* the practice which had brought unpopularity to Sarı Ali Efendi.[43]

All sorts of Muslim Ottomans were assigned the right to regular payments from state income in return for various services, or for other reasons. Such assignments—"wages"—snowballed. They had become an important factor in the Ottomans' chronic financial troubles. The obvious way to deal with the matter seemed to be to check the master lists of assignments against each individual's documents, which the assignee had to present in person, and then to strike off from the lists the names of all those who were not actively serving.[44] Naima points out that this procedure of striking off names [*kat-ı erzak*] is really not feasible. The whole history of Islam and the combined experience of wise men show that the official who attempts such an abrupt change courts disaster, perhaps even death, and that even so he does not achieve the desired end. Naima sees no reason to cite examples from remote periods of history. As recently as the time of Köprülüzade Mustafa Pasha, a general audit [*yoklama*] was carried through. The result was that even Mustafa Köprülü, despite all his signal services to the state, incurred the hatred of rich and poor alike.

It is natural for people to ask what else can possibly be done except to strike from the payroll the names of those who are irregularly assigned fixed stipends from the customs receipts and from the other farmed revenues. Naima has searched out an answer to this question from the standard histories of the past, and presents his recommendations in the form of an essay (VI, 310–15).

The standard books of Muslim law conceive of the Muslim treasury as containing four categories of funds,[45] and the disposition of these funds to various classes of Muslims is carefully worked out. After summarizing the main headings of this system, Naima notes that it is more honored in the breach than the observance. With the passing of time, many differing practices have become established. For example, most of the ulema now are paid from funds that go with their posts—that is from endowments—and in this way they are not direct charges on the state. Most other individuals who—in theory—have a just claim on the Muslim treasury are cared for from the Ottoman customs-farm income. But for a grand vezir to resolve to strike from the lists of the Sublime State those rich assignees—and the relatively insignificant number of poor assignees—at one stroke is not enlightened patriotism. Rather, full attention must be paid to a number of considerations so that state expenditures may be reduced and regularized successfully.

The first step is not to strike off the names of individuals now holding assignments, but to stop making new assignments. Together with this, when an assignment now on the books falls vacant through the death of the assignee, it should be allowed to lapse and should not be reassigned to another would-be beneficiary.

Secondly, trading in these assignments should be forbidden, just as it is forbidden to trade in *evkaf* paper.

If these steps are taken, in a few years many outstanding assignments will lapse; those funds will consequently accrue to the treasury. On the other hand, if a quick "review" should be attempted, it will prove very difficult to catch defrauders. It is generally known that many wealthy men, men well able to support their own households, have obtained an assignment of public funds to practically every person in their households, even to their slaves.

Under these circumstances, if a general review of the assignment lists is attempted, it is perfectly plain what will happen. Each holder of a certificate [*berat*] will be required to present it in person. Those who illegally hold certificates will put each of these certificates into the hands of some poor, crippled old man and send him to present the berat to be validated as his own. He will answer all the questions put to him, the government will be defrauded, and nothing will have been accomplished. When the audit is over and done, the rich will still be getting their illegal state-aid. This in turn will again entail cutting the amount that can be given to the deserving poor. They on their part will resent this—and the would-be reformer will end up by being cursed by the rich and poor alike.

The only sure means of attack is to go at the matter gradually. For example, Osman Paşaoğlu was ordered to check the list of those drawing assignments from the customs revenue, and what happened? Not only did he add to the rolls the names of ten or fifteen of his own followers, but apart from that he also gained everyone's ill will. And he is not a unique example.

An anecdote of an old Turkish king serves to illustrate Naima's point. This king had no beard. In consequence, he required that all males in his kingdom should be clean shaven. Fortunately he had a very wise vezir who persuaded him to grant three years' time so that the measure could be put into effect gradually. First, the adolescents just sprouting beards were ordered to shave. Then, after a time, eunuchs were required to shave on the grounds that people did not like for them to wear beards. This measure received the support of the clean-shaven adolescents. Finally, after an appropriate time, it was ordered that all men should shave. The men who had tough beards all protested, but the adolescents, those with sideburns, and the scanty-beards all supported the measure and so the day was successfully carried on an issue that would have caused great difficulties had the vezir not gone at it gradually.

The moral is obvious. Righting the finances is, in the last analysis, principally the grand vezir's responsibility. If a well-intentioned grand vezir attempts to do this by precipitate measures, his successor will soon undo whatever the former may have accomplished. But if that grand vezir profits by the experience of the past, if he dissimulates his real intentions and moves toward his goal gradually, he will succeed. From this it follows that a padishah who wishes to achieve reform should pick a suitable grand vezir and give him free rein (VI, 315).

Finally Naima wishes it to be understood that what he has had to say refers specifically to the assignments which are made on the customs funds and to the other alms for the Muslim poor, and that the question of reforming the payrolls of the janissaries, *sipahis,* and other military corps is beyond the scope of this essay.

These matters are treated in Suhrawardi's essay which was Sultan Selim I's guide, the essay which Naima has mentioned in "the preface to this book." If he succeeds in translating it, full details can be found there.

59. **Kadızade's Followers**

Under the year 1066 (began October 31, 1655) Naima treats "The Affairs of the Followers of Kadızade Efendi," prefacing the account of the incident with a valuable summary of the most important movements in seventeenth-century Ottoman history.[46] Presumably this summary is Naima's own (VI, 239). Its main points are as follows:

The questions at issue between the orthodox ulema and the Sufis in Islam are very ancient. They go back to the time of the orthodox caliphate. Thereafter, in many of the successor states and in Baghdad and Cairo the conflicting claims of these two parties frequently resulted in bloodshed. No permanent resolution of the differences between the two schools has ever been reached, and in every age notoriety-seekers revive the old quarrels.

So it was in the Ottoman empire when Kadızade, representing the orthodox ulema, renewed the quarrel with the Sufis who were led by Sivasi Efendi.

The biographies of these two men, and anecdotes about them, are now given, Sivasi Efendi having died in 1049 (1640), some four years after the death (early summer, 1636) of his opponent Kadızade who was the son of a kadı from Balikesir.

These two men were completely at odds with each other. They differed on no less than sixteen unresolved points. Their personal differences were magnified by their respective followers who were literally at each other's throats, especially during the confusion of the earlier part of Murad IV's reign. Then Murad IV asserted himself, took the matters of state into his own hands, disposed of Recep Pasha, his grand vezir, and appointed Tabanıyassı Mehmed Pasha. With this Murad IV had begun his campaign of forcibly restoring order throughout the state, closing coffee-houses, forbidding the use of tobacco, and so on. Kadızade supported the sultan in these measures and thus garnered great favor for himself. But it was not unqualified favor: Sivasi Efendi also had his share of honors from the sultan. This greatly intensified the rivalry between the two men.

Following Kadızade's death, his followers reached new heights of intolerance. They flatly condemned all innovations (all practices not ascribed to the Prophet and to the men of his time) and went so far as to declare that all Sufis are actually heathen. In consequence, the Muslim community was split into two factions.

Here Naima goes back a few years to point out that from the start of Murad IV's reign it had been the followers of Kadızade who possessed the power and the wealth, the good things of this world, and that this was in sharp contrast to the position of the Sufis. The orthodox ulema then had a hand in all that went on in the palace and could use their influence in all affairs. In the palace they were particularly strong among the halberdiers and the gardeners (*bostancıs*), and among the gatemen (*kapıcıs*). Representatives of all these corps frequented the ulemas' lectures, and it came to be said that such and such a man had made his fortune "in class." Through these men Ustuvani Efendi was in touch, first with the black eunuch and eventually with the valide sultan over whom he gained influence. He also was able to avail himself of the help of the imperial intimates and so came to have a hand in appointments, promotions, transfers, etc. Through secret communication with the imperial favorites he gave advice on all measures, saying that a measure was or was not in the interests of the religion and the state. He sold his influence, and so became wealthy as well as powerful. Eventually no one dared stand against him and the palace eunuchs and servants who served as his go-betweens.

In the end, the eunuchs were dealt with and the ulema lost a portion of their power when Boynuyaralı Mehmed Pasha became grand vezir. But they bided their time until, when Limni and Bozca were lost, they had the opportunity of causing his fall by contending that the Ottoman failures were due to the fact that the grand vezir and the mufti were Sufis and that all troubles were the result of "innovations."

Mehmed Köprülü had been grand vezir for scarcely a week when the orthodox ulema again stirred up a riot in the city. They planned to pull down all the *tekke*s, to kill all the dervishes who refused to renounce Sufism, and finally to get the sultan to forbid all "innovations"; for example, no mosque was to have more than one minaret.

Köprülü found that gentle measures were useless, so he obtained the sultan's permission to execute all inciters to riot. In the event, however, he contented himself with exiling three of the principal ulema to Cyprus; they were Ustuvani, Türk Ahmed, and Divane Mustafa.

Naima now appends a series of amusing anecdotes: One of the

orthodox, when questioned by a wit, had agreed that trousers, underdrawers, and spoons should be abolished. Were they not all "innovations"? He also agreed that this step would throw the spoon makers out of work (it being of no consequence that henceforth everyone would dress like a bare-bottomed desert Arab) and proposed that the spoon makers might turn to producing non-innovation goods such as tooth picks and prayer beads. His interlocutor agreed that such a solution would do for ordinary people, but stumped the orthodox when he asked to what the people of Mekka and Medina, who also lived by producing innovations, could turn.

Hüseyin Maanoğlu had described one of these orthodox bigots to Naima. This man professed to be a rigid orthodox ascetic in public, but in private led a life of ease and pleasure. Maanoğlu, who was his intimate friend, once taxed him with this inconsistency between preaching and practice. He replied that what one did in private was of no importance as long as one's public example did not mislead others.

Following this comes a statement that the late seyhülislâm Yahya Efendi once said that it was only after he became seyhülislâm that he came to appreciate what good points there are in the practice of this sort of dissimulation and pretense. Here Naima somewhat self-righteously observes that the good points of hypocrisy are only apparent and not real. In the long run it is better to keep as far away as possible from opportunities, and to give them no more rein than is absolutely necessary. This is well illustrated by a recent exponent of opportunism, Vani Efendi, whose story will be related under the events of Köprülüzade Fazıl Ahmed's grand vezirate.

Naima closes this long section with two more anecdotes, the first about Vani Efendi and how he rationalized his indulgence in forbidden luxuries, and the second reverting to the followers of Kadızade. At the start of Mehmed Köprülü's grand vezirate, various important Sufis had sought the help of Hanefi Efendi against the aggressive hostility of the hypocritical orthodox ulema. Hanefi Efendi compared these followers of Kadızade to a great shade tree with branches everywhere. One branch was the *bostancıs* of the Palace, one branch reached from the halberdiers' headquarters all the way to the imperial palace. A third, and a great, branch was the people of the market place. Several important ulema of the time were present at this meeting—for not all of the ulema approved of the radical orthodox faction by any means. One of these, Mustafa Efendi of Bolu, said, "Gentlemen, among the men of God the 'sword of the hidden' is well known. If you were to turn to *it* for your revenge . . . ," and quoted sura 8 verse 25 of the Koran.[47]

Less than a week later, Köprülü had banished the orthodox leaders.

60. **On History**

In contrast to the unsystematic fashion in which Naima scatters the "results" of his study of history through his text is the careful presentation he makes in Preface One of his ideas on why and how history should be written.

From Naima, I, 4–8

In the mirror of the innermost hearts of men of keen intellect, it is clear and plain and manifest and evident that the science of history and the science of biography are the quintessence of instruction and information and the elixir of excellent qualities and intellects, an august and great study whose subject is of universal utility, for it teaches those happenings and lessons which have been manifested in the world, from the earliest periods up to this very moment, and it expounds those occurrences, good and bad, which have transpired in creation from the covenant of Adam to this time. History has ever been common fare among the peoples and nations, a subject esteemed and of currency within the various estates and millets *of mankind, approved and sought after by great sultans and noble rulers, the solicitude and desire of outstanding men of fame and renowned men of wisdom.*

It is a science of much usefulness, appertaining to the common good. It increases the liveliness and the keenness of scholars' intellects, makes the attentiveness and penetration of wise men broader, puts the commonality into possession of the story of what has happened aforetime, and gives the elite knowledge of secrets which would otherwise be concealed.

Those erudite adepts who successfully sail to an understanding of the essential truth of this shoreless sea [*of history*] *attain jewels of perfection and pearls of truth. They discern how many secrets are concealed in that divine necessity which causes the epochs to change and the times of climates and lands to alter. They discern how it was that, in ancient times, the expansion of the girdle of power occurred, and how changes of condition began to appear among the peoples of the past. They became men of clear insight, informed as to what are the causes and the springs of action which foretell and which bring decay and decline to the civilization of mankind and which show that a state, a society of men, is taking the road to expiration and death. Now in the time of a state's prosperity, that state possesses certain inherent qualities—if not native characteristics as in the case of a human being—and it is to these qualities that the history of particular incidents is subordinate. They are the root to which all its traditions and achievements go back. Those principles and usages and rules of policy which are determined in the very nature of prosperity, the innate differences between the several regions, and the special nature of the social order of human beings are—all of them—ever ready at the hand of a logically minded man who loves history. For him they serve as standards of judgment and as useful analogies.*

Certainly a man who will not be content with primitive traditions about what happened in history is not a man to be duped by sophistries and silly stories and tales of every sort. Instead, he will infer what is missing on the basis of the data which he has, and will derive the lacking circumstances from those with which he is acquainted. Through much experience and much application he reaches a point at which he can foresee what will be the results of actions, provided he understands the men who do those actions, and can comprehend the affairs of great men, provided he knows what the causes prior to those affairs were. In his mind's mirror, the consequences of circumstances become clear, and the forms of good and evil distinct, as if by intuition.

Thus the science of history is the pursuit of a glorious pathway, noble of purpose and full of usefulness.

Of the great men of ancient days, how numerous were the historians who collected and recorded the marvelous events which took place within the four corners of the world and the odd happenings of that past age of this world of vicissitudes! Subsequently, century by century, able and talented writers, poets as well as writers of prose, recorded the events that transpired, kind by kind, and the happenings in the commonwealth which they saw or of which they heard. And so, in the science of history the compositions—detailed and abridged—which they added to those compilations which they themselves had had from their forefathers came to be more and more numerous. And confusions of words led to differences of meanings.

Thereafter, how numerous were the sagacious men who, in their turn, in order to confirm the old tales and to correct the accounts which had been appended to them, painstakingly and carefully collected the best works of this science of history, separating the valuable from the worthless and choosing out the least corrupt accounts! These men then wrote books which are monuments worthy of the favorable regard of the masters of criticism.

In Arabic, among the best of these later histories are Ibn abi Ḥajalah's Sukkardān al-Salaṭin,[48] *Ḥalabi ibn al-Shīḥnah's* Rawḍ al-Manāẓir,[49] *and Maqrīzī's* Khiṭaṭ *and* Kitāb al-Sulūk.[50] *Above all there is Ibn Khaldûn the Maghribi's Arabic history* ʿUnwān al-ʿIbr fī Dīwān al-Mubtada' wa-l-Khabar, *a book whose preface alone is one entire volume.*[51] *It is an incomparable treasure-trove, full of gems of learning and pearls of judgment. Its author—a marvelous man—has surpassed all historians. His book is concerned with what took place in the Maghrib, but into his preface he introduced the whole of his learning.*

Of Persian works which are similarly received and prized, there are Ghiyān al-Dīn Khwāndamīr's Ḥabīb al-Siyar[52] *and the* Nigāristān-i Ghaffārī.[53] *And in Turkish are the late Hoca's translation of Lārī*[54] *and Âli's* Künh el-ahbar.[55] *Kâtip Çelebi, well known by the name of Hacı Kalfa, wrote the history of the Ottoman state from the year* 1000 A.H. to 1065, *entitling his book the* Fezleke; *in truth it is a pretty historical compilation, not overly supple in phraseology or overly saccharine in its expressions, and without affectation.*[56] *Kara Çelebizade Abdülaziz Efendi likewise made a delightful compilation of the affairs of the Ottoman state. His style is full of beautiful expressions and is not verbose. He began at the start and epitomized, bringing his work up to* 1067 [A.H.]

As for special histories—well-known or obscure—histories restricted and limited to particular countries or individual states—of these there is no end.

Excursus

There are certain vital conditions and important rules for those who record events and for those scholars who write history:

First: *They must be reliable in what they say, and must not make foolish statements or write spurious tales. If they do not know the truth about any particular question, they should address themselves to those who have fathomed it, and only then put down whatever they have ascertained to be the fact.*

Second: *They should disregard the disquieting rumors which are gossiped about among the common people. Instead they must prefer the reliable, documented statements of men who knew how to record what actually did happen. How often do men of feeble intellect base their conclusions upon their own fallible imaginings! Although the actual nature of many events, and also the causes behind them, are well known to those who had a hand in them, such writers nevertheless spread abroad erroneous or completely unfounded accounts. Every century has many writers who accept widely spread popular rumors of this sort as fact and write them down for posterity without even once having examined into them.*

Third: *Whatever the sphere of human life to which the question of which an historian is treating belongs, he should not be content simply to tell the story but should also incorporate useful information directly into his narrative. It is of no great consequence merely to recount campaigns and seasons of repose from campaigning, arrivals and departures, appointments to office and removals from office, and peace and war. Rather, historians ought first to inform themselves, from those who have proper information concerning the question in hand, of what was the divinely ordained condition of any age in history; of how, in a given century, the affairs of men were going forward, and in what direction; of what ideas and counsels were predominating in problems of administration and finance—in short, historians must first ascertain what it was that men thought and what it was over which they disagreed, what it was they believed to be the best course in the conduct of war and in making terms with the foe, what were the causes and the weaknesses which were then bringing triumph or entailing destruction. Then, after an historian has ascertained all these things, he should present his findings on the basis of their reliability. When this has been accomplished, later readers will be able to avail themselves of the different benefits of experience's teachings. But simple annals, devoid of these useful features, are in no way different from so many* Hamza-names.[57]

Fourth: *Historians should speak frankly and fairly, ever mindful of the powers of the common people. They should not be fanatic or boastful or falsely modest or scandalous. If they must shield or praise some friend who does not deserve it, they should not exaggerate beyond the bounds of reason.*

And if, to attain their end, they must criticize and censure great men of praiseworthy works, they should never be unjust. In any case, they must take care to present the real nature of the question, regardless of what it may be.

Fifth: *Historians should abandon overly varied phraseology and overly obscure expressions. Instead they should choose easy phrases which the reader can fully grasp. Words that send one to the dictionary, and constructions and phrases fit for a style book are not suitable for a history. As if the author's purpose were to display his talents and eloquence and mastery of rhetoric in a work designed for the learned. . . .*

Sixth: *Historians should quote in full any interesting correspondence of which they can get hold, useful anecdotes, verses and prose passages appropriate to the topic, works of unusual content, and epigrams.*

Seventh: *Historians, provided that they understand the science of planetary influences, should record the influences which conjunctions had upon affairs, the changes of years, eclipses, and the other ascendants, scientifically. If they are able to search out the visible effects which—as people assert—the great, active astral bodies, those bodies which release the angels who are charged with the execution of God's decrees, have exerted upon the tribes of the past, if they are able to search out conditions which these forces manifest in the social order of the state and then insert concrete proofs in their account of events, then they will have displayed their authority as experts in astrology.*

It is necessary and important for all historians to conform to the above conditions insofar as they can, just as the writer of [*this*] *history has conformed in certain particulars.*

From Naima, I, 8

Naima's Verse to History

'Tis this that the clever masters recount:
The study of history is nothing less than a treasure of gold.
A man beholding gold and jewelries takes pleasure therefrom;
So study and history are insights' light.
Books are like a boon-companion—mute;
He knows the condition of Heaven's ancient wheel.
As if he had the very tongue of fortune,
He bares secrets to those forbidden to know them.

So history has become the interpreter of the age.
It reports events but has not tongue.
Sometimes it speaks plainly of ways of conduct;
It opens speech about the struggle of the Good of mankind.
Sometimes it tells of men of fame,
Of the tales of the sultans of the earth.
Sometimes it reveals the secrets of the state.
It describes the condition of the kingdom and the people.
The old and the new, ancient and modern
Become known and plain through history.
Because history is a noble science,
Noble men's nature has delighted in it.
The master of this science is a man of penetration.
He who is ignorant of it is uninformed.
Had the teachers of old not written history,
Who would know of the conditions of the past?
For the brethren to come did the great men of old
Make the sweets of the present to exist.
Men of wisdom, taking pity on those yet to come,
Toiled to compose their book.
This is proper, that noble patrons
Should strive towards writing such a work.
Let them find an author of graceful style
And show him their favor.
Let him be able to write in a convincing fashion,
Let him fix and set down events effectively,
Thus it becomes a means to win men's prayers hereafter.
The work becomes an expounder of the noble litany.

61. **Why Write History?**

History is important, not in itself, but because it is of use. It has "universal utility." It "appertains to the common good." It produces "men of clear insight" among those who are familiar with it. It enables men to "foresee the result" of actions which they contemplate taking. It provides the reflective man with "standards of judgment and useful analogies."

Above all, in times of crises, responsible officials such as the grand vezirs for whom Naima wrote should have at hand a reliable statement of world history, that is, of the history of pre-Islam, Islam, and the Ottoman period of Islam (with the emphasis ascending in that order). Such a statement will prove to be both a bulwark and a true "guide to what to do."

There is no reason to suppose that Naima and his patrons were not sincerely convinced that the study of history would help save the state, but it was not until the height of the Tulip Period (1718–30) that the official movement to foster the knowledge of history gained momentum. The licensing of the Müteferrika press provided one means. Such figures as İshak Efendi, Salih Efendi, and Esat Efendi gave their full support.[58]

62. How to Write History

By setting up a seven-point ideal of how history should be written, Naima courts the risk of having his practice judged on the basis of his own preaching. That judgment is not particularly unfavorable. He holds that an historian should observe the following precepts:

1. Tell the truth and substantiate it.

2. Disregard the false tales current among the common folk.

3. Not content himself with "simple annals" but enable the reader to draw the moral for himself.

4. Not be a partisan, regardless of his own views.

5. Use plain language and not sacrifice clarity to literary affectation.

6. Limit himself strictly to appropriate embellishments (verses, quotations, etc.).

7. Discuss astrology only when he can prove that astrological causes had certain established results.

We shall be in a better position to evaluate Naima's success in observing his seven principles when we have surveyed his sources and how he handled them. The standards he sets for himself are high. Within the limits of his time and place he unquestionably did try to measure up to them. We have seen that he attempts to tell the truth without overly elaborate varnishings, even when he deals with the Edirne revolt in the preface for Ahmed III and Moralı Hasan Pasha. He uses as much material as he can lay his hands on, and he indicates his sources, as will appear.

He spurns rumors and folk-tales. When he introduces one for effect, he indicates that it is a tale and not fact.

Ample examples have been given to show that he attempted not to content himself with "simple annals" but to enable the reader to draw a "helpful" conclusion. According to today's taste, it will seem that Naima did little to free himself from the limitations of the annals-form, and this is true from the viewpoint of the modern concept of history. But when judged by his own criteria, in his own time and place, Naima compiled a good record.

He subordinated his own views to a great degree, even to a regrettable degree from our point of view. His partisanship is almost entirely restricted to the prefaces where it is not out of order.

Language affected to the point where it obscures the meaning is found only in Naima's long quotation from Nabi. The literary extravagances of various sources have been toned down sufficiently not to bother the businesslike reader to whom Naima addresses himself.

Embellishments are refreshingly few, even in the prefaces, when compared with the bulk of classical Ottoman literature.

Although himself accused of practicing astrology, which, for that matter, was implicitly believed in by practically all educated men of the time,[59] Naima seldom introduces such material into his work.[60]

It would be foolish to say that Naima attained his goal in all particulars. It would be entirely unjust to say that he did not try for the goal, or to deny that he gained a real measure of success.

Raşid notes that he himself follows Naima's example in matters of the division, organization, and presentation of material, in adopting the annals framework as his system, in presenting some narratives complete in one section, breaking other narratives up into sections and articles, and also, where necessary, in carefully contradicting false accounts and practicing fairness.[61] Naima's own ideal, not always attained, was that each event should be recounted in its chronological place, broken up into sections—each with its own title—and followed by comment upon the narrative.[62]

For a final judgment of Naima's upon what is permissible and proper in the writing of history, we turn to his remarks upon the death of the poet Nef'i—describing how Nef'i had come to Istanbul from his native Erzurum, become an official scribe, won fame during Ahmed I's reign (1603–18), and gained even greater fame and imperial favor under Murad IV who ascended the throne in 1623 (III, 234–5). But Nef'i was overly fond of satirizing the great. Murad IV liked informality in his private social relations, and this fact resulted in his personally hearing Nef'i read several of his satires on well-known figures. Finally, one day when the sultan was at Beşiktaş in the Sultan Ahmed I Palace and was amusing himself by leafing through a satirical collection by Nef'i, a storm came up and the palace was struck by lightning. The sultan at once tore up the book and had it burned, removed Nef'i from his official post, and vowed never again to indulge in reading or listening to satires.

Eventually Nef'i regained favor, but in overweening pride he ventured to write a satire against the vezir Bayram Pasha. When, in a moment of relaxation, the sultan asked Nef'i if he didn't have some new satire, Nef'i produced this one which the sultan later showed to Bayram Pasha. And the sultan gave permission for Nef'i to be executed.

To this account Naima adds:

Such is the chronicler's account. The tale which is commonly known among the people is this: Sultan Murad, at a private gathering of his friends, said to Nef'i, "Give us a satire on Bayram Pasha," and insisted till Nef'i had to comply. Then when Bayram Pasha learned what Nef'i had done, he came to the sultan and said, "After this satire I have no influence or standing among the people. My padishah, grant me permission to kill that evil man!"—insisting until the sultan gave him permission to execute Nef'i (III, 235–6).

This popular tale is completely unfounded, and the chronicler's account is closer to the truth, for it is not sensible to suppose that kings would permit vezirs to be satirized. But however it was, Bayram Pasha was permitted to kill Nef'i. When Bayram had returned to his own palace, he sent a man to fetch the poor Nef'i, whose blood the ulema of the time, in accord with the verse [*in Persian*],

> That poet who speaks tumult,
> that man named Nef'i,
> By all four schools is his killing as proper as
> the killing of the adder,

had declared should be lawfully spilled. He came in all innocence. After Bayram Pasha had mightily upbraided him, he imprisoned him in the wood-room of the palace where he had him strangled and thrown into the sea. The ulema and the grandees of the time were delighted at Nef'i's death, and it was especially those outstanding figures whom Nef'i's sharp tongue had wounded that praised Bayram Pasha for this matter.

I have heard from Maanzade Hüseyin Bey that when Bayram Pasha commanded that Nef'i should be taken, when men went out [*to do it*] *the çavuşbaşı was Crooked-neck Çavuş! He was a Turkish fellow. He confronted Nef'i and said, "Come along, Nef'i Efendi. Out in the wood-room there's a man who will fix up a satire. Come on and see!"—and so he pulled Nef'i's leg in the Turkish fashion. Nef'i despaired of his life and said, "Go on, you damned Turk, tell me the worst," and rudely vilified the great vezir.*

Those who do not act on the maxim [*Arabic*] *"The Muslim is he from whose hand and tongue other Muslims are safe" cannot rest at ease on the maxim* [*Arabic*] *"A man's safety is in guarding his tongue."*

The truth is this: lampooning is a calamitous and a shameful deed, and to spend its changes and accidents upon a stupid man is even more worthy of censure and altogether worse. Those who take this turning gain no good fortune or success, but the end of most of them is ruin in this world and deserved torment in the world to come. Of this there is no doubt.

Calm speakers, the great poets who are the keys of the hidden treasures, do not approve the soiling of the page of the paradises and the seed of eloquence with evil acts which cause reproach (III, 235–6).

63. **Conclusion**

By this point, reference has been made to almost every statement and every hint in the whole of Naima's work that will cast any light on the question of what sort of man he was. His personality does not emerge clearly, but his convictions do. Unless one wishes to maintain the unlikely proposition that Naima consistently forged a set of attitudes that he did not in fact entertain—that he deliberately and successfully fools the reader from start to finish—it follows that Mustafa Naima was all of the following:

He was a man of practical realism, not a fanatic, not markedly an opportunist. He prized common sense and he believed that criticism should and could be constructive. He was completely a child of his own times. As such, he was unreservedly loyal to the Ottoman way—to his faith, state, and civilization. He affects to prize personal integrity highly, and there is no evidence that he, himself, was not both honest and courageous.

These assertions are not difficult to support. The man who frankly admitted that the Ottoman system ca. 1700 only approximated Islam's theory, and who was content that this should be so, was not a fanatic. Everyday common sense certainly should be attributed to one who feels that even Mustafa Köprülü had been ill-advised to incur unnecessary unpopularity, that a practical politician will foresee the danger of allowing too many elements to become his enemies at one time, and that there is nothing to be gained in the long run from being overly harsh. Sycophancy cannot be seriously charged against a man who flatly admits that no power on earth can completely eradicate human greed and foolishness. The historian who recognizes that old songs and stories may be used as propaganda devices to revive popular morals and that news of the sultan's intimate bearing and moods spreads through Istanbul and even the whole empire swiftly and with great effect, is a practical man with something constructive to offer. The same is true of Naima's plea for physical and intellectual training, and especially so of his encouraging assurance that just as it would take only a few determined men to ruin the state so too it needs only a few resolute men to turn the tide.

There is little to indicate that Naima was a man of enthusiasms, much to stress his practical, resolute realism. The long plea for making use of the "means at hand" is not that of a dogmatic man, a stickler for custom and tradition. Naima frankly admits that times change and we must change with them, that "words which do not comport with the time in which we live should be abandoned." It is the practical, even the disillusioned, man who counsels "easy does it," recognizing that, in his time of crisis, enlightened patriotism was not to try to remake the world overnight, but rather to accomplish at least something without upsetting the apple cart.

The attributes of leadership—skill, courage, honesty, pride, loyalty, and good judgment of men—that Naima recognizes, his belief that an individual's real loyalty to faith and state would naturally entail the curtailment of that individual's greed and personal ambition, his feeling that it is personal loyalty and steadfastness that redeem the practice of *intisap* and that in the absence of such loyalty politics is a dirty game—all these show what store Naima would put upon integrity. It is basic if success is to be obtained, and it is as indispensable in a sultan as it is in others. When men are men of integrity, contention ends and the weakness of the state diminishes. Integrity failing, contention holds sway and not even the most lofty figures are safe. If the sultan chooses a dependable grand vezir and gives him his head, the sultan has done enough.

Honest men know that pride goes before a fall, that a stitch in time saves nine. The honest historian does not hesitate to express a candid opinion of rich men who milked the state by getting their families "on relief," or of the military and their failings, and the orthodox ulema and their hypocrisy. The practical realist makes it clear that these strictures do not apply to all the ulema, but the honest historian has the courage to admit flatly how insecure life in Istanbul has become and to point out plainly the wrong he feels Mehmed IV did to Kara Mustafa Pasha.

Underneath this temperate candor is a strong loyalty to his "own" —to Islam, religion, state, and civilization—the Ottomans' faith and state and the "Ottoman Way."

For practical purposes world history is simply the history of

Islam. At this time of crisis, Islam *is* the Ottoman state, and every good Muslim should realize this and act on that fact.

Muslim history is the entire frame of reference. Early Muslim history is the idealized golden age when "justice was pure and equity unmixed." Islam will inevitably triumph because it is "better." The Ottoman system needs much reworking and restoration, but it is good and uniquely good and is destined to endure.

The degree of conviction with which Naima, or any of his contemporaries, embraced any one of these ideas can never be fully known. Nevertheless, one may rest assured that men of Naima's circle, the liberal upper-class Ottomans of the day, subscribed to these beliefs, used them as criteria upon which to judge men's actions, and truly believed that it was in these ways that loyal Ottomans should serve faith and state with their wealth, bodies, and minds.

NOTES

1. Compare P. Wittek, *Rise of the Ottoman Empire*, p. 3.
2. The Köprülü grand vezirs:

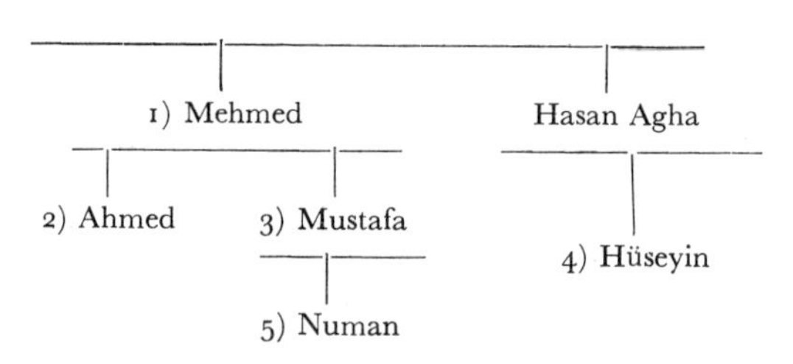

3. The war ending with the peace of Karlowitz, 1699. The Ottomans counted fourteen summers of campaigning, beginning with and including 1109/1683, Raşid, *Tarih*, II, 431. Naima, I, 62, says that the war began fifteen years before 1108/1698–7, that is, in 1093/1682, the year when Kara Mustafa Pasha opened hostilities prior to the attack on Vienna.
4. Kurat, *Prut Seferi*, II, 493–537, 653–74.
5. This accounts for his nickname, Amcazade, "Uncle's son."
6. Raşid, II, 408 seq.
7. *GOR*, VI, 658 seq.; Zinkeisen, *Geschichte*, V, 3–236. See also *İA*, VI, 346–50; Rifa-'at A. Abou-El-Haj, "Ottoman Diplomacy at Karlowitz," *JAOS*, Vol. 87, No. 4 (December, 1967), 498–512.
8. That Köprülü's views, as expressed in this preface, were soon forgotten is indicated by the stereotyped assertion in Raşid, II, 433, that Köprülü had made peace with the Europeans "against his will."
9. "The means at hand" is a key phrase in Naima's defense of Köprülü's course. It included making peace with the European powers and also the unpopular, though necessary, reforms he instituted at home.

10. "The task of summoning": that is, in the spreading of Islam.

11. Yusuf Nabi, died 1124/1712, *GOW*, 237–9. His *zeyl* (appendix) is to the *Siyer* of Üveys ibn Mehmed (Veysi) who died in 1037/1628, *GOW*, 152–4.

12. Written ca. 1400. For an English verse translation, see Süleyman Çelebi, *Mevlid-i şerif*, F. Lyman MacCullum, trans.

13. *İA*, I, 672.

14. Naima, I, 27–44; Section II–B–1 and II–B–2 of the outline given above.

15. Kâtip Çelebi, *Düstûrü'l-'amel*. For a German translation, see W. F. A. Behrnauer, *ZDMG*, XI (1857), 110–32.

16. For an excellent account of his life, see A. Adnan Adıvar, *Osmanlı Türklerinde İlim*, pp. 115 ff. Autobiographical material is available in Kâtip Çelebi, *The Balance of Truth*, G. L. Lewis, trans. pp. 135–52.

17. This was written only three years before such a man materialized—the elder Köprülü. It is possible that the *Düstûrü'l-'amel* was a part, and even an important part, of the political and propaganda groundwork which paved the way for Mehmed Köprülü's appointment as "absolute" grand vezir.

18. The child Mehmed IV, accession 1648.

19. The life of man and of the state falls into three ages: growth, maturity, and decline —conditioned, in each case, by the strength or weakness of the individual's physique. Each age has its peculiar symptoms, and each age will respond only to the remedies appropriate to it.

The correspondence between man's four humors and the state's four component classes (*erkan*) is as follows:

1. The men of the faith (ulema)—the blood.
2. The men of the sword (*asker*, the military)—the phlegm.
3. Merchants (*tuccar*)—the bile.
4. Peasants (*raiyyet*)—the spleen.

20. This study makes no pretense of tracing the ultimate origins of these, and other, ideas of Naima. His debt to Ibn Khaldûn is evident. See Ibn Khaldûn, *The Muqaddimah*, Franz Rosenthal, trans. Our interest is not in where ideas originally came from, but in what ideas Naima actually held and advocated.

21. Kınalızade Âli Efendi, *Ahlak-ı Alâî*, III, 49. Kınalızade Âli Efendi died in 1572. See *İA*, VI, 709–11. For other versions of the circle of equity, see Walter L. Wright, *Ottoman Statecraft*, p. 64, n. 4, p. 119, n. 19; Lybyer, *Government*, p. 20.

22. *Mulk*: sovereignty, especially God's sovereignty; *devlet*: State, earthly sovereignty.

23. *Kitāb al-sulūk li-ma'rifat duwal al-mulūk*, a history of Egypt from 577/1181 to 844/1440.

24. Unidentified.

25. See *GOW*, 113.

26. On *fütüvvet*, see the article "Futuwwa" in *EI*[2], II, 961–9, and the bibliography cited therein.

27. *EI*[2], II, 964.

28. *EI*[2], II, 968–9.

29. The section's title is: "A Number of Prefaces, Containing Rare and Important Points Drawn up to Set Forth Completely Several Useful Principles and Major Precepts which have to do with Natural Processes and Fundamental Qualities, for the Purpose of Expounding those Several Established Peculiarities which Govern Regular Customs among States and Peoples and in the Natures of Mankind."

30. "Men of the pen": here in the broadest sense, ulema and scribes; Naima, I, 50.

31. "Conclusion of the Discussion," Naima I, 58–65.

32. Zinkeisen, *Geschichte*, V, 200 seq.

33. In his preface Müteferrika states that Naima's popularity was in part due to the fact that he was free of the "overly-sweet" style; Naima, I, xv.

34. İbrahim Müteferrika, a Hungarian by birth and education, was better informed. He stresses that the Ottoman state now has to deal with Christian foes whose firearms are not to be compared with those of the foes against whom earlier Muslim states fought, Naima, I, ix–x.

35. "Bowl-men," that is men enrolled as janissaries and drawing pay but rendering no military service.

36. On *nasihat*, see Wright, *Statecraft*, p. 17.

37. Firari Kara Mustafa Pasha, to be distinguished from two other well-known bearers of that name: (1) Kemankeş Kara Mustafa, the last grand vezir to Murad IV, and (2) Maktul Kara Mustafa, the grand vezir executed by Mehmed IV after the failure at Vienna in 1683.

38. *GOR*, VI, 25, 187–8.

39. Compare Naima, III, 453, where Naima reproduces verbatim Kâtip Çelebi's opinion that Murad IV was the best of the sultans after 1000 A.H.

40. Sivasizade Abdülbaki, great-grandson of the original Şemseddin Ahmed Efendi. Mehmed III had brought the family to Istanbul, in part because he wished such holy men to accompany the army, "for luck." (See a portion of the original firman reproduced in *SO*, III, 400, without indication of the source.) In Istanbul the family maintained a station in the upper ranks of the ulema for more than a century. Abdülbaki was born in 1614, and died in 1710, only six years before Naima's death.

41. A favorite spot for excursions, near the head of the Golden Horn.

42. Naima, II, 392 seq. See also *GOR*, V, 66, 660 seq.

43. Literally, "the cutting off of supplies."

44. The process of checking was called *yoklama*.

45. 1. alms, 2. booty, 3. taxes, 4. unclaimed estates.

46. Naima, VI, 227–41. See also Kâtip Çelebi, *Balance*, pp. 132–4. The episode of Kadızade's followers marks a distinct decline in intellectual activity among the Ottomans, Adıvar, Osmanlı *İlim*, pp. 105–6.

47. "And be afraid of temptation (*fitnah*): the evil doers among you will not be the only ones on whom it will light," J. M. Rodwell, trans., *The Koran*, p. 377. The word *fitne* (here better rendered as "going astray" or "disobedience") to the Ottomans had come to mean "rebellion" or "evil doing."

48. Ibn abi Ḥajalah died in 1375.

49. Ibn al-Shiḥnah died in 1412.

50. Al-Maqrīzi died in 1442; for a reference to his *Sulûk*, see Section 42.

51. Ibn Khaldûn died in 1406.

52. See C. A. Storey, *Persian Literature*, I, pt. 1, 101–9.

53. Al-Ghaffāri died in 975/1567–8, *ibid.*, 114–6.

54. Al-Lārī died in 979/1571–2, *ibid.*, 116–7.

55. *İA*, I, 304–6.

56. See Section 68.

57. Impossible folk-tales. See the references listed in *GOW*, 13, note 1.

58. See Müteferrika's license and petition in Ahmed Refik, *On Ikinci Asır*, No. 121, pp. 89–91, and No. 122, pp. 91–4. The men who aided Müteferrika were distinguished intellectual leaders. (This was a far cry from the situation a few years earlier when the orthodox ulema had officially put history beyond the pale.) They were İshak Efendi, son and brother of şeyhülislâms, and himself şeyhülislâm by the time Naima was published (*GOW*, 286); Esat Efendi, well known as a poet and translator, a former kadi of Galata (*SO*, I, 332); Musa Efendi, an important Mevlevi şeyh; and Sahib Efendi, usually referred to as Pirizade, who not only became şeyhülislâm, but is also famous as the first Ottoman translator of Ibn Khaldûn's Mugaddimah.

59. *İA*, I, 682–8; Enver Ziya Karal, *Selim III. 'ün Hatt-ı Humayunları*, pp. 1–2.

60. But see his Preface II, Naima, VI, appendix, 26, 43–4. Naima allows the astrological material in his sources to stand, Naima, II, 80. Raşid, like Naima, minimizes astrology.

61. Raşid, I, 10.

62. Naima, Preface II (separately paged), VI, 4.

CHAPTER THREE
Work

64. **Time Span**

The *Tarih-i Naima* records Ottoman history from the beginning of 1000 A.H. (October, 1591) to *Şevval*, 1070 (April, 1660), a time span of seventy-one years and seven months in the Muslim calendar.

Volume: Müteferrika edition	Volume: 3rd edition	Dates, A.H.	Dates, A.D.
I, 701 pp.	I, 462 pp.	1000–1015	October, 1591–April, 1607
	II, 451 pp.	1016–1038	April, 1607–August, 1629
	III, 460 pp.	1039–1050	August, 1629–April, 1641
II, 711 pp.	IV, 460 pp.	1051–1059	April, 1641–January, 1650
	V, 452 pp.	1060–1064	January, 1650–November, 1654
	VI, 441 pp.	1065–*Şevval*, 1070	November, 1654–April, 1660

The first third of the work (volumes I and II of the third edition) covers thirty-nine years, more than half of the entire time span, while the final third (volumes V and VI), in an equal number of pages, covers only eleven years. As he approaches his own times, Naima's account thus becomes distinctly more detailed.

The time span of this extant work, however, is not that which Naima says he covered. He asserts that his history is in two volumes, Volume One from 982 to 1065 (1574 to 1655) and Volume Two from 1065 (1655) to "the present," that is, to about 1704.[1] This does not fully coincide with the assertion of Şehrizade (see Section 13) who calls "volume I" all that Naima had put into final form—that is, the section ending with 1070 A.H., the terminus of the printed Naima—and states that Naima's rough draft "volume II" continued from 1070/1660 to 1110/1698–9.[2]

Evidently we must allow for some exaggeration on Naima's part. Did he intend to begin with 1574 (the accession of Murad III), but never find time to complete this earliest section (to 1591)? Did he incorporate his day-book into his rough draft "volume II" only as far as 1110 A.H.? In any event, we are left to ask what became of what Şehrizade calls the rough draft "volume II" (from 1070 to 1110/1660 to 1698–9).

One can only conclude that at the time of Naima's death, or perhaps at the date when he ceased work as a professional historian, his final draft was substantially the *Tarih-i Naima* we have today. There is no trace in the manuscripts of any section preceding the beginning of the published work, and no sure trace of the later, unfinished section.[3]

Thus the text that has always been regarded as Naima's complete work covers a shorter time span than its author says he planned to treat. It is a case of a grand design only partly executed. According to Naima's original plan, both the beginning and the end are missing.

65. **Contents**

In form, Naima's history is a typical Muslim chronicle. Hence the modern mind finds its arrangement exasperating. Ideally, each year is a unit and each "event" under that year is a single entry. In the case of an important "event" such as a major campaign, the account will be presented in several sections. Usually, but not invariably, those sections are grouped in a block. For the most part, an important block of this sort stands at the head of the events for that year.

In the case of an "event" that is prolonged over several years, the reader must skip from year to year, from block to block, in order to assemble Naima's whole story. There is little cross-reference, little of résumé to help one keep the story's thread unbroken. Frequently the emphasis on military operations almost entirely obscures the larger picture.

Unlike his predecessors, Naima did not append at the end of each year's events the biographies of important men who died during the course of that year. Instead, he introduced those biographies directly into the text at appropriate places. Traces of the older plan still remain, however. For the year 1000 A.H., for some reason, the obituaries are included as they are in the *Fezleke*. The same is true for the year 1066 A.H. (VI, 242) and the following years. As we have seen, both the very earliest and the latest sections of Naima are unfinished; this seems to be one particular to which Naima was never able to attend. Like traces are to be encountered throughout the text. At the end of his last entry under the year 1023 (began February 11, 1614), Naima notes (with his own boyhood memories as source): "It should not be forgotten that the said imperial son-in-law Mehmed Pasha who became grand vezir after Nasuh Pasha was killed—as has been described above—is that wise vezir ordinarily known as Okuz Mehmed. He now lies buried in Aleppo in the *tekke* of Şeyh Ebu Bekr" (II, 136; see also p. 175).

The location of this addition to the text is puzzling, for the item to which it is appended is not "The Execution of Grand Vezir Nasuh Pasha and the Grand Vezirate of Mehmed Pasha," an item that has occurred in its proper place in the narrative of 1023 (II, 123), but is instead the Turkish text of the second of two treaties which Naima here gives.[4] The position of this note can only be explained by assuming that it skipped Naima's attention when he was arranging his final draft, and that originally it had been appended to the final obituary in the series of obituaries which, in Naima's source, closed the account of each year.

The death of a sultan is the occasion for a summary of that sultan's life and works, for lists of his grand vezirs and of other important official figures of his reign, and for a tabulation of important men who died during the reign.

The chronicle begins during the reign of Sultan Murad III and breaks off during that of Mehmed IV. Thus it treats of eight sultans (nine reigns):

1. Murad III (his death, I, 106)
2. Mehmed III (his death, I, 365)
3. Ahmed I (his death, II, 154)
4. Mustafa I (deposed, II, 160)
5. Osman II (killed, II, 208)
6. Mustafa I (second reign: deposed, II, 263)
7. Murad IV (his death, III, 444)
8. Mehmed IV (still reigning when the chronicle breaks off).

The subject of the chronicle is simply "Ottoman history." *Ottoman* here is not a geographical term. The intent is not, in the first instance, to treat all the peoples of the Ottomans' empire. Interest rather is focused on the Ottomans themselves, that is, on the dynasty and its Muslim Turkish servants. Reference to non-Ottomans, whether to the non-Muslims of the empire or to non-Ottomans (Muslim or not) abroad, is ordinarily made only when the Ottoman story itself naturally entails it.[5]

Ideally the central thread of this sort of chronicle is the story of the sultan's life, especially of his official actions. However, with the exception of Murad IV, the sultans treated by Naima largely kept to their palaces. Thus the only central thread that they provide is a narrative of what happened in the orbit Istanbul-Edirne, including riots, politics, ulema politics, and such major turning points as the murder of the valide sultan, and the installation of Mehmed Köprülü as grand vezir. This Istanbul-Edirne narrative is the theme of Naima's chronicle, insofar as one is justified in speaking at all of a central theme. Entwining about that theme and at times completely obscuring it are several major threads. The earliest of these threads is the yearly account of events on the European frontiers of the Ottoman Empire.

Early in the work comes Mehmed III's Egri (Erlau) campaign in 1596.[6] Thereafter with few exceptions, such as Osman II's Hotin campaign in 1621,[7] Naima's account of the fighting in Europe and in the Black Sea area has to be presented largely without the sultan as the central figure. As the years go by, the thread of events leads Naima to decrease his emphasis on the fighting in Europe, but it of course remains a major thread throughout the book.

A second important thread is the fighting in the east, above all the wars with Persia. With Murad IV and Shah Abbas this thread truly becomes dominant. A third important thread and one frequently tangled with the second is Naima's account of the Anatolian disorders, the *celâlî* revolts, which began—or recommenced—with the seventeenth and continued more or less in an uninterrupted series until the nineteenth century.[8] Events in Arab lands are treated as they are caught up on one or the other of these two threads or as they are involved in the Istanbul story of political intrigue. Apart from this, the Arab world is largely neglected.

With the start of the Ottoman conquest of Crete in 1645, there enters a fourth important thread (IV, 123). Operations in Crete, still incomplete when Naima breaks off, are recorded in great detail. They account for almost one-sixth of the entire bulk of Naima. It is only with them that Naima begins to pay particular attention to the Ottoman fleet.

Interesting tales are given prominence when they come naturally into the narrative. They are seldom dragged in by the ears. The criterion of what is interesting, of course, is what interested the Ottomans themselves. An excellent example is Naima's account of the tragic end of the Jewess "Kira," one of a family dynasty of women, who served as go-betweens linking the women of the palace with the outside world.[9]

Detail is a virtue in Naima's eyes. As he deals with the wars in Europe, such men as Stephen Bocskay and Bethlen Gabor, relatively remote figures from the point of view of traditional European history, appear at length. But detail is a virtue only in matters near at home. Thus even the Hapsburg emperors are scarcely mentioned by name while the sovereigns of Western Europe are almost ignored. Once again one notes that *the* criterion is Ottoman history, written for the Ottomans. This, of course, seems no more parochial to us than the ordinary western view of history would have seemed to an educated Muslim of Naima's time. Naima adds nothing to what the Ottomans already knew of Europe, East or West, and gives us scarcely a word to show that he himself had ever paid the least heed to, or even heard of, any Europeans except those with whom the Ottomans came into direct contact.

66. **Naima's Own Composition**

In the preceding sections "Naima" has been used almost as a generic term. Everything that is "in Naima" is there because he deliberately included it in his final draft, but only a relatively small proportion of that final draft was his own composition. He was a compiler, more critical than many, but still a compiler. The few sections that he appears deliberately to have refused to reproduce from his sources would evidently not have added significantly to the total.

One can single out with reasonable assurance of accuracy the important sections that Naima actually wrote himself. These sections alone "are Naima" in the strict sense, and it is only on them that one's judgment of the author should be formed.

Important sections from Naima's pen are the following:

I, 273, 286	concerning Tiryaki Hasan Pasha
II, 27	memories of Aleppo
II, 86	Hafız Pasha's courage
II, 136	memories of Aleppo; Öküz Mehmed Pasha's death
II, 174–5	memories of Aleppo; Öküz Mehmed Pasha's tomb
II, 208–9	why the murder of Osman II should be treated in detail
II, 384	on *Hurûfî* magic
II, 392–3	caution: concerning the exchange of verses between Murad IV and Hafiz Pasha
II, 435	criticizing belief in magic
II, 441 *seq.*	supplementary remarks of Husrev Pasha (presumably Naima's)

III, 170 *seq.*	on Murad IV
III, 179–80	on Maanoğlu
III, 235–6	Nef'i's execution
III, 385–6, 388	concerning Diyarbekir (perhaps Naima's personal memories)
III, 391	on Maanoğlu's sister
III, 419	personal memory of the old Ankara janissary
IV, 13–14	on the execution of Silihdar Mustafa Pasha
IV, 104 *seq.*	the desert chief Assaf
IV, 295–6	on Naima's father
IV, 310–11	on Hezarpare Ahmed Pasha
IV, 333	why Sultan İbrahim was executed
IV, 335–6	contrasting Şarih al-Manarzade and Kara Çelebizade
IV, 346	Şarih al-Manarzade's partiality
IV, 351	the *sipahis*
IV, 401–11	on Sufi Mehmed Pasha
V, 69–70	reproaching the ulema
V, 103	the Old Valide and the aghas
V, 107	why Şarih al-Manarzade's tales about the Old Valide are suppressed
V, 115–6	on the murder of the Old Valide
V, 282–3	on Kâtip Çelebi's *Düstûrü'l 'amel*
VI, 119 *seq.*	boyhood memories of Aleppo
VI, 148	on Maanoğlu's partisanship
VI, 224	on the son of Defterdar Mehmed Pasha
VI, 227 *seq.*	the Followers of Kadızade
VI, 242	on Kör Bey
VI, 249	personal knowledge of Istanbul
VI, 275–6	on Firari Kara Mustafa Pasha
VI, 299 *seq.*	on Kara Hüseyin Agha
VI, 308 *seq.*	on *kalem* reform
VI, 361	on Evrengzib's story
VI, 363–4	On Kara Çelebizade's death
VI, 383	on the use of Vecihi's history
VI, 420	on the son of Şami Numan Efendi

67. **Kinds of Sources**

Naima's sources fall into two main groups, written and oral.[10] The written are by far the more important but the oral are not negligible. The same assertion holds for Naima's predecessor, Şarih al-Manarzade (see Section 70). There is little difficulty in distinguishing between the oral informants of the one and the other, but this is not always true with regard to their use of written sources.

Naima reproduces almost the whole of Şarih al-Manarzade's unfinished chronicle. He seemingly always notes the fact wherever he omits anything that was included in the Şarih al-Manarzade manuscript. Şarih al-Manarzade, in his turn, is said to have incorporated the chronicle of Hasanbeyzade into his work. Hence much of Naima is a version of a version of Hasanbeyzade.

The remainder of this chapter is devoted to an over-all review, dissecting Naima's history into its original parts. That process will not be carried through in detail; only a general survey is desired. We shall consider the following:

1. The relationship between the extant *Tarih-i Naima* and Kâtip Çelebi's *Fezleke*
2. Şarih al-Manarzade's contribution
3. The written sources that Naima and Şarih al-Manarzade used
4. The contribution of Hüseyin Maanoğlu to the *Tarih-i Naima*

68. **The Fezleke**

The relationship between the published texts of the *Tarih-i Naima* and the *Fezleke* of Kâtip Çelebi is close and perplexing.[11] The printed *Fezleke*, a very poor edition,[12] lacks Kâtip Çelebi's preface. Nonetheless one may be certain that the *Fezleke* basically is a précis of Hasanbeyzade's chronicle of Ottoman history. The *Fezleke* covers from 1000/1592 to 1065/1654. Certain years, particularly at the close of the work, are almost "empty." These are the years after Hasanbeyzade's own chronicle breaks off. Naima and Şarih al-Manarzade managed to fill in those years with some success. To illustrate this, and also to provide a skeleton-index for the *Fezleke* (which has none in the printed edition), the following table is presented:

Year (A.H.)	*Fezleke*	*Naima*
1000	I, 2	I, 66
1001	8	76
1002	15	85
1003	38	100
1004	59	135
1005	77	147
1006	98	178
1007	108	194
1008	123	221
1009	135	234
1010	146	251
1011	178	297
1012	196	327
1013	242	390
1014	256	412
1015	275	441
1016	289	II, 2
1017	304	27
1018	321	62
1019	334	84
1020	339	88
1021	345	93
1022	351	99
1023	355	114
1024	368	136
1025	374	141
1026	383	150
1027	390	160
1028	397	171
1029	399	174
1030	402	186
1031	II, 8	207
1032	31	245
1033	46	283
1034	65	343

Year (A.H.)	*Fezleke*	*Naima*
1035	72	356
1036	94	401
1037	100	416
1038	108	433
1039	114	III, 2
1040	128	49
1041	138	74
1042	150	134
1043	153	165
1044	162	217
1045	169	250
1046	184	286
1047	189	319
1048	193	328
1049	214	418
1050	222	457
1051	223	IV, 4
1052	224	11
1053	226	20
1054	233	65
1055	239	116
1056	273	186
1057	294	229
1058	312	251
1059	341	383
1060	357	V, 2
1061	367	45
1062	380	181
1063	382	260
1064	392	373
1065	397	VI, 2
1066		127
1067		246
1068		315
1069		380
1070		429

With the exception of the obituary notices at the end of each year in the *Fezleke,* practically every entry found in the *Fezleke* in the earlier years is also found, often in somewhat more verbose but not necessarily more informative version, in Naima. Some material found in the *Fezleke* has been dropped in Naima.[13] Probably it was lost during the years when Şarih al-Manarzade's rough draft "fell into the cupboard of oblivion" (see Section 22), and was never restored by Naima. As for the *Fezleke's* biographical notices, some, but not all, were inserted into Naima's text.

Thus the present text of Naima contains a version of almost the entire *Fezleke.* Much of the time, especially in the earlier years, the two chronicles have one wholly identical structure. Section titles and the sequence of sections coincide. But this is not the whole story of the connection between the two works, for Naima also used the *Fezleke* as one of his direct sources, as one of the standard histories from which he took and incorporated sections to supplement Şarih al-Manarzade's manuscript. This use of the *Fezleke* is more common in the later years.

Before any statement on the connection between Naima and the *Fezleke* can be substantiated, a great amount of editing will have to be accomplished. There is not a single critical edition of any Ottoman historical work of the seventeenth century. Of the Istanbul editions, those by Müteferrika—and those reprints based on his editions—are the best, but even they leave much to be desired. If any scholar or group of scholars ever undertakes this task, it is probable that he or they will soon conclude that most Ottoman historical works treating the eleventh century of the hegira are versions of, or at least incorporate, one basic account; that this account is the "History of the Year 1000" (*Tarih-i sene-i elf*);[14] and that the general foundation of this account is a series of extracts from Ottoman official records (see Section 75) to which the individual "authors" have added opinions, anecdotes, personal experiences, and extracts from other versions of the same basic chronicle.

The *Fezleke* and Naima are both erected on one version of that chronicle.[15] Apparently this version is what is meant by Hasanbeyzade's history[16] although that version extends beyond the supposed date of Hasanbeyzade's death.[17]

Comparison of Naima and the *Fezleke* shows that their common underlying version of the "Chronicle of the Year 1000," in the form that it had reached before Kâtip Çelebi began to write, already had made greater or less use of the following: (1) Hasanbeyzade's chronicle, (2) Abdülkadir Topcular Katibi, (3) Âli, (4) Peçevi,[18] (5) Mehmed ibn Mehmed, (6) Vecihi, plus many other less important sources, particularly oral informants who are mentioned in connection with specific events.

In consequence, failing critical examination of manuscripts, the connection between the *Fezleke* and Naima is to be formulated thus: 1. large sections of the two works are parallel versions of a yet earlier version of the "Chronicle of the Year 1000"; 2. Naima also makes use of the *Fezleke* as a source from which to supplement Şarih al-Manarzade's manuscript.

69. **Şarih al-Manarzade: Life**

Naima's predecessor, Ahmed, "the son of the commentator of al-Manar," was born at Amasya, the son of one of the ulema, Mehmed Abdülhalim Efendi.[19] The son grew up in Amasya, entered the ulema corps, and taught there before coming to Istanbul with his father. Meantime the father had written a commentary to the *Manār al-Anwār*, an Arabic work on Muslim canonical jurisprudence. Because of this he was called *şarih,* or commentator, of the *Manār,* and his son received the *künye* (by-name) of Şarih al-Manarzade. As Naima was to do subsequently, Şarih al-Manarzade also had inserted into his chronicle certain information concerning his own father. Thus we know, for example, that the father died on Friday, the 17th of *Ramazan*, 1051/December 20, 1641.[20]

Mehmed Efendi's commentary helped him attain an upper-level ulema career. The son describes with obvious pride how his father received the highest ranking ulema office which either of them was ever to hold, kadi of Bosnia.[21] The appointment was made in early 1046/midsummer, 1636, toward the end of Murad IV's reign, while Mehmed Efendi was in Istanbul "at liberty," that is, seeking an appointment. He replaced a kadi who had been discredited by a revolt in Bosnia, and the son asserts that his father was instrumental in dealing with the aftermath of this revolt.

It was necessary to change defterdars as well as kadis in Bosnia. The new defterdar proved to be İbrahim Efendi of Peçevi, the well-known Ottoman historian,[22] with whom Şarih al-Manarzade's father was thus personally associated for some time.

Şarih al-Manarzade himself spent most of his life in Istanbul. He died in 1067/1657, long before Naima arrived there.[23] In Şarih al-Manarzade's career, the following points are established. At Istanbul he became a protégé of the Hoca Efendi family, the descendants of that famous mufti, Sadeddin, who plays an important role in the earlier years of Naima's chronicle. Between 1598 and 1694, members of this family had no less than twelve terms as mufti. They were the third family in the Ottoman state in the nineteenth century, next after the Köprülü family which was second only to the dynasty itself. Their history remains to be written.[24]

The first clue that Şarih al-Manarzade gives us of his own career is that about 1644–45 he had become the deputy of Mufti Ebusaid's *arpalık* at Gallipoli.[25] Mention of this is introduced as Şarih al-Manarzade relates stories of his personal contact during 1644–45 with İslam Giray, a member of the Crimean royal family who that same year (1054 A.H.) became han of the Crimea.

When Bahadur Giray Han, İslam's elder brother, had died in *Şaban* 1051/October 1642, İslam had not been made han. Instead, his younger brother Mehmed Giray was elevated to the throne while he himself went to live at Hisar-i sultanî (Çanakkale) as a "guest of the government," that is, as a hostage.[26] Three years later Mehmed Giray was deposed and banished to Rhodes and İslam did become han.[27]

During the time that İslam Giray and his steward, Sefer Agha, were at Çanakkale, and Şarih al-Manarzade at Gallipoli, they were all familiarly associated. Şarih al-Manarzade, doubtless with his patron's approval, may have been active in furthering İslam Giray's intrigue to gain the office of han. İslam in return presented Şarih al-Manarzade with a fine copy of Hafiz's *Divan* in the handwriting of the late Bahadur Giray Han.

Kemankeş Kara Mustafa Pasha, the grand vezir, had opposed İslam's ambitions. When the grand vezir was executed, 21 *Zilkade* 1053/January 31, 1644, İslam's steward at once went to Istanbul to pull strings. He was not immediately successful. For a time İslam himself was banished to Rhodes, and this must have interrupted his contact with Şarih al-Manarzade. However, after his eventual investiture in Istanbul, Şarih al-Manarzade saw the new han and preserves an interesting account of Sultan İbrahim's conduct during that ceremony.[28]

This episode at least shows that Şarih al-Manarzade was a trusted, confidential retainer of Ebusaid, enjoying the favor of the Hoca Efendi family. They continued to support him. In mid-*Şaban* 1059/late August 1649, he was appointed to the Perviz Efendi *medrese* in Istanbul.[29] He was transferred to teach at the Ahmed Pasha *medrese* in Istanbul in late *Recep* 1062/late July 1651,[30] and to another *medrese* in the first decade of *Rebiyülevvel* 1065/October 12–21, 1654.[31] Perhaps this last appointment was to the Davud Pasha *medrese* where he was, Şeyhi says, at the time of his death in 1657.[32]

70. **Şarih al-Manarzade: Work**

Şarih al-Manarzade's history existed only in the rough draft that Naima worked over. A copy of it is reported in the catalogue of manuscripts on Turkish history in Istanbul.[33] Naima ordinarily refers to his own predecessor as "the chronicler." Not infrequently, as we have seen, Naima differs from that predecessor. This is not astonishing, for Şarih al-Manarzade's version of the Ottoman seventeenth-century chronicle was fundamentally an ulema version, more properly the Hoca Efendi family version, and although it does not represent rigid ulema opinion of the Kadızade school, nonetheless it must at times have been quite uncongenial to Naima personally.

Şarih al-Manarzade's name first appears in Naima's chronicle under the year 1018/began April 6, 1609 (II, 82). He is last mentioned in 1065/began November 11, 1654 (VI, 31). Thus he had brought his unfinished history up to about three years of his own death. His principal written sources were a version of the "Chronicle of the Year 1000" (see Section 68), and the history by Abdülaziz Kara Çelebizade. The chronicle he reproduced in its entirety.

Abdülaziz, an ulema opponent of the family that Şarih al-Manarzade supported, is usually introduced to be criticized.

Şarih al-Manarzade wrote largely of his own time and included many stories that informants had given him at first hand. Some of these he reproduced in a very lively fashion, even mimicking accents and speech impediments.[34] He also included official lists of ulema promotions and a good measure of ulema polemic. Some of the latter Naima eliminates.

Şarih al-Manarzade's notes, that is, his additions to the Chronicle, were written in the margin of his copy, the copy that came into Naima's possession. Larger additions were on separate sheets. Thus Şarih al-Manarzade's manuscript, which Naima used, should be conceived as an unbound stack of sheets—not even a bound register.

Naima does not hesitate to deal rather roughly with his predecessor at times. Nevertheless, we have to thank Şarih al-Manarzade for much of the present text of Naima. Some of the praise that Naima has received, even the praise for his insight into human psychology, by right should go to Şarih al-Manarzade. In many passages the whole material is Şarih al-Manarzade's, without any doubt, and should be so cited.[35] In many passages it is also possible to cite Şarih al-Manarzade's own informant by name.

In sum, this predecessor's contribution to the work known as *Tarih-i Naima* is scarcely less important than that of the compiler by whose name the work is called.

71. **Formal Histories**

In the foregoing sections mention has been made of a number of formal histories that entered into the *Tarih-i Naima*. In addition to the *Fezleke,* to those works that were used in the common chronicle-source of Naima and the *Fezleke*—Hasanbeyzade, Abdülkadir Topcular Katibi, Âli, Peçevi, Mehmed ibn Mehmed, and Vecihi—and to Şarih al-Manarzade's frequent source, Abdülaziz Kara Çelebizade, several other formal histories appear in the finished *Tarih-i Naima.* In particular, Naima directly cites the following:

1. Telhisi Abdi, died 1689, the Ottoman historian sometimes called the first official historian.[36]

2. Mehmed Halife (Has odalı), whose work may be the foundation of the later part of Naima.[37]

3. İsazade Efendi, an historian who lived until 1750, but whose work (beginning with 1065/1654) must have been available in part to Naima by 1703–4.[38]

The above are far less important than are the standard histories from which Naima's predecessors had cited, and of which Naima also makes direct use himself, as follows:

1. Hasanbeyzade, said to have died 1046/1636.[39] Naima's last citation from his history is for the year 1033/began October 25, 1623, although it is usually stated that Hasanbeyzade's work reaches only to 1032.[40]

2. Abdülaziz Kara Çelebizade, the ulema opponent of the Hoca Efendi family, died 1068/1658.[41]

In addition to these, mention is made of many individual informants of whose accounts Naima gets hold in one or another way. Various other Ottoman works are mentioned at least once, and many works of general Muslim literature are referred to in passing.

It is striking that Naima seems to make no use of Selânikî or of Kemaleddin Mehmed Taşköprüzade's *Tarih-i Saf*.

Since editions or manuscripts of only a few of the sources cited in the *Tarih-i Naima* are available, it is futile to attempt more than this general tabulation of Naima's sources. From that listing one concludes that Naima and his predecessors among them had access to a vast amount of material, that no one of them used the whole of that material systematically, but that the *History of Naima* is nonetheless a rich and valuable compilation. It also should be stressed that in many sections of Naima the identity of the original source is so plain and the probability that the source is being reproduced verbatim is so high that it should be cited not simply as "Naima," but, more accurately, as "X in Naima."

72. **Maanoğlu: Life**

Naima's only important verbal informant, Hüseyin Maanoğlu, is an interesting figure in his own right. He was the son of the great

Druze Emir Fakhr al-Dīn whose career in Syria and in Italy is well known (see Section 21).

Hüseyin Maanoğlu was born about 1625.[42] In 1043/1633–4 Küçük Ahmed Pasha defeated Fakhr al-Dīn II, whom the Ottomans had long regarded as a dangerous rebel.[43] It was resolved to exterminate the Maanoğlu family in the Jebel Druze. The Emir Fakhr al-Dīn and his two sons, Mesud and Hüseyin, were brought to Istanbul. His sons were considered "young and capable of being taught,"[44] that is, they could be made into good Ottomans, and young Hüseyin was placed in the Galata Saray school. Soon thereafter Murad IV left Istanbul for the Erivan campaign (III, 242). On the day of his departure he received Fakhr al-Dīn and his two sons. Apparently they were not in danger. Murad, however, soon changed his mind and in *Şevval* 1044/began March 20, 1635, an order for the father's execution reached Istanbul. He was beheaded and the son Mesud strangled, but Hüseyin—because he was the younger, according to Naima (III, 242)—was spared.

He had become one of the privy pages in the Galata Saray. From there he advanced to a post in the *has oda* of the Palace sometime before Murad IV's death in 1640 (III, 392). Under Sultan İbrahim (1640–8), he became steward of the treasury, and under Mehmed IV he added to this the post of confidential secretary (III, 392; see also 179–80).

Then on 6 *Recep* 1066/April 30, 1656, Maanoğlu "went forth" to become a *kapıcıbaşı* (VI, 164). This was a high post and in the same year he rose higher, going as Mehmed IV's ambassador to India (VI, 208–9). Traveling by way of Basra in the company of the returning Indian ambassador, he proceeded to India, but arrived only after the death of Shah Jahan (VI, 410–11). The situation in India—a war of succession—seems to have led Maanoğlu to return to Istanbul almost at once. The fact that in the meantime Mehmed Köprülü had become grand vezir may also have contributed to his desire to hurry home. He arrived home in 1069/1659, bringing from Murad-Bakhsh, the son of Shah Jahan and the man who had received him, a letter, which contained nothing more specific than "compliments and expressions of friendship" (VI, 410). When the sultan asked Maanoğlu what was the most wonderful thing he had seen in India, the diplomatic Ottoman son of rebel Druze emir replied, "My noble padishah! Of all those marvels that which seems finest to me is that we were able to get back to this paradise-like land" (VI, 411).

Soon after Maanoğlu Hüseyin had left Istanbul, Mehmed Köprülü had become grand vezir. Maanoğlu owed his position and his wealth to all those forces that Köprülü was henceforth to control. Hence one assumes that Maanoğlu after his return to Istanbul not only held no official position, but lived, as Naima says he did, quietly till his death in 1102/began October 5, 1690 (III, 179–80; also see Section 21, above). He was probably no more than seventy years old, although Naima portrays him as a very old man.

Whatever the relationship between Maanoğlu and Köprülü may have been, Maanoğlu retained his fabulous fortune, all of which must have been amassed during his own career in the Palace and as *kapıcıbaşı*. After his death, his widow brought that fortune to her next husband, Sipahi Agha Salih, and Salih was even called Maanoğlu.[45]

73. Maanoğlu: Work

Hüseyin Maanoğlu's contribution to the contents of the *Tarih-i Naima* is much smaller and less important than Naima's assertions would lead one to hope.[46] Maanoğlu adds nothing to Naima's story of the former's father and brother. In the same way, Maanoğlu contributes nothing to illuminate one of the most enigmatic narratives in Naima's entire chronicle, the story of a nameless Maanoğlu daughter—presumably Hüseyin Maanoğlu's own sister. She enters "history" in connection with the execution by Murad IV of a Nakşbendi şeyh, Şeyh Mahmud of Urumia, at Diyarbekir in 1048/1638–9 (III, 389–92). Şeyh Mahmud's *tekke* at Diyarbekir had become the center for a large following that spread throughout Kurdistan and Iran as well as the Arab regions of Diyarbekir. The Ottomans probably viewed him as a potential threat to the dynasty, analogous to the founder of the Safavid line in Iran. Şeyh Mahmud had seemingly behaved well to the sultan when Murad IV was en route to Baghdad, but on the return trip Murad had him put to death immediately upon reaching Diyarbekir.

Naima states that his narrative here follows Şarih al-Manarzade who in turn is based on the *Fezleke* (III, 368). Naima, however, objects to a *tafsil* (section of detail) that Şarih al-Manarzade has appended, giving two reasons for Murad IV's execution of the şeyh (III, 387–91). One of these reasons Naima considers sound: Şeyh Mahmud was so powerful that he threatened to become the founder of a new dynasty. But Şarih al-Manarzade's other explanation is called into question. This passage Şarih al-Manarzade had given on the authority of an oral informant, Silihdar Pasha Reisi Hüseyin Efendi, a confidant of Murad IV and an eyewitness of what had befallen Şeyh Mahmud. Presumably Şarih al-Manarzade knew the informant personally (Naima, III, 386).

The story was that when Fakhr al-Dīn II and his sons were carried to Istanbul and the attempt was made to exterminate the Maanoğlu family in the Jebel Druze, a grown daughter of Fakhr al-Dīn II escaped and got to Diyarbekir disguised as a man. Passing as a man, she claimed to know alchemy; her father had taught her how to change base metals into silver and gold. Şeyh Mahmud had become convinced of her power, and when, on Murad IV's approach, he went to greet him at Aleppo, he took with him some gold she had made as a present for the sultan. The sultan was interested. This process promised to be a means of financing his campaign. When he himself reached Diyarbekir he advanced the alchemist and her şeyh sponsor a sizable sum of money for necessary supplies. He also left a *kapıcıbaşı,* an experienced metallurgist, to supervise operations. After Murad had gone on toward Baghdad, the alchemist lived a life of ease on her supply money. It was only with great difficulty that the *kapıcıbaşı* finally made her set to work. The results of the experiment were unsatisfactory. This news was reported to the sultan at Baghdad and that fact explains his anger at the şeyh. Both he and the Maanoğlu girl were executed.

Naima rejects this story completely on grounds of common sense (III, 391). All people who have claimed to possess the alchemist's secret have concealed it. They do not boast of it to sultans. Nor was Şeyh Mahmud so foolishly impractical as to boast of this to Sultan Murad IV. As noted, Naima has no word of comment on this episode from Hüseyin Maanoğlu who could hardly have been ignorant of the story that some member of his immediate family had in some way or other angered or defrauded Murad IV at Diyarbekir and had been executed there.

Naima does at once tell a story illustrative of unsuccessful alchemy and this story is on Maanoğlu's authority (III, 392). It concerns a giant of a Moroccan who, soon after Murad had returned from Baghdad and Diyarbekir, performed an alchemical experiment at the palace, again under the *kapıcıbaşı's* supervision. The Moroccan failed and was put to death. Later, after Murad IV's death, Maanoğlu found in the imperial treasury, in Murad's private safe, the amalgam that had been produced in this second trial. It had been put away in a box by itself.

In connection with these two alchemical passages it is interesting to recall that Salim, writing soon after Naima's death, accused Naima himself of being a "chemist" (see Section 20).

Maanoğlu's years in the treasury made him somewhat of a jewel expert.[47] Apparently he also had traveled to Egypt, perhaps while still in the Palace service or less likely on the return voyage from India.

Naima was personally familiar with Hüseyin Maanoğlu's fine private library and names three particularly choice volumes from it—a *Şahname,* a copy of Âli's *Künh ül-Ahbar,* and one of the *Tarih-i Vassaf,* all of them in the hand of the famous copyist and chronogram author Cevrî Çelebi. Maanoğlu also provides Naima material for his death notice of Cevrî.[48] The same statement on Cevrî makes it clear that Naima was personally acquainted with several of the better, privately owned libraries in Istanbul.

Perhaps Maanoğlu's single most interesting contribution to the *Tarih-i Naima* is the following passage. Maanoğlu is not named there, but it is evident that he is its inspiration if not its author. It is introduced in connection with a discussion of Sultan İbrahim's notorious extravagance.

From Naima IV, 293–4. Year 1058/1648

Good Counsel

In the books of the sages of old it is said that it is not wise for a ruler to become particularly fond of luxury goods and deluxe wares that originate in enemy lands, or even fond of those which are obtained from regions belonging to other states, lest through the ruler's fondness for them those goods become the mode so that because of them the money and wealth of the state go to other lands. Instead of this, rulers ought for the most part to show a fondness for those rare goods that are produced in their own lands so that wealth will not be scattered from their kingdoms to other places.

To those who object that the money received from customs duties is of benefit to the state, we answer as follows:

If those who import goods from other kingdoms and sell them to us spend the money that they thus receive on goods produced in the Muslim lands, on goods that they need, then the currency remains in the [Ottoman] kingdom. In this case, customs duties collected time after time are to be considered a benefit. An example of this is the Frankish crew [European merchants] who bring woolens and other cloth and who buy from the Muslim lands mohair and galls and alum and potash and lye and similar permissible wares. It is not only [the cargoes of] ships which are disembarked at Smyrna, Payas, Sayda, and Alexandria, but also esedi altın.[49] *Even the regions of Ankara and Sayda and Tripoli [in Syria] and the whole of the Jebel Druze are full of this wealth.*

But as for the money spent by us on sables and other sorts of expensive furs that come from the regions of Moscow, those accursed ones spend nothing for goods produced in Muslim lands. In the same way, how much wealth goes for goods from India while the people of India buy nothing from the Ottoman provinces! Indeed, what we have to sell is not what they need. They are in the position of having incomes so large that the supposed utility of customs collections is not even a moral deterrent to them, while they spend nothing in other lands because they have no needs. Hence the wealth of the world gathers in India, just as it does in the Yemen because of its coffee, and wealthy men there are like Croesus.

74. Method

Naima's method deserves our attention. He is particularly interested when various sources give him alternate or conflicting accounts of the same event. Such cases are frequent. Naima ordinarily reproduces all the available accounts verbatim, pointing out that they are in conflict. He then may attempt himself to decide which account is the more probable, or he may leave the question open, taking refuge in the old formula, "God alone knows."

But not too much was left to God. Where possible, Naima sought out men who could help him. Examples noted are the following:

1. A son of the former *defterdar* Saçbağı Mehmed Pasha from whom Mehmed Köprülü had extorted the former's ill-gotten gains. The son, a poor old man and a Kadriye dervish, was known to Naima.[50]

2. Kör Bey, the son of another *defterdar* Mehmed Pasha, still alive in Naima's time and serving as a *kapıcıbaşı*. Kör Bey lived in the mansion of the former gümrükçü Ahmed Pasha, near the Sultan Süleyman mosque.[51]

3. A son of the late Şami Numan Efendi, still alive and the owner of property in Beykos (VI, 420).

Such mention of living figures naturally comes principally in the last years of Naima's history, and these figures out of the past whom he knew personally must have been, of course, quite old men.

Naima's mention of such informants indicates that he took real pains to assemble material for incorporation into his history. It also emphasizes how true it was that Ottoman Istanbul, for a man in the upper ranks of Muslim society, was actually a small town where everyone knew and was known by everyone.

The point that sets Naima in a class apart from most chroniclers is his readiness to assume that any or all of his predecessors may be in error on a given point. We have seen that he did not hesitate to question Maanoğlu's judgment, much as he respected his memory.

Even more illustrative of Naima's praiseworthy readiness to question other's opinions and to probe other's motives is the treatment he gives to Şarih al-Manarzade. Şarih al-Manarzade had been a partisan in ulema politics; the successes and fortunes of his patrons, the Hoca Efendi family, had colored his view. Naima recognizes this and frankly makes allowance. At one point Naima states, "The late chronicler [Şarih al-Manarzade] was one of Behâi Efendi's clients, one of his friends who made up his *meclis*. Therefore he notes in the margin of the history . . ." (IV, 335). Naima accuses Şarih al-Manarzade of partisanship against various of the other ulema, for example, Yahya Efendi,[52] and frequently Abdülaziz Kara Çelebizade (IV, 335). Such accusations are substantiated in the sense that Naima proceeds to reproduce the passage of Şarih al-Manarzade to which he takes exception.

There are other cases in which Naima edits Şarih al-Manarzade. Apparently he always feels obligated to warn the reader that this is the case, and to justify himself. So, when editing Şarih al-Manarzade's attack on the followers of Kadızade, Naima states, "At this juncture the chronicler censures and reviles all the şeyhs who were brethren of Kadızade. Since in his strictures on them he exceeds the bounds of moderation, his illogical statements have been digested and are reproduced [only] as a means of carrying [the narrative] forward" (V, 45). Again Naima does not reproduce Şarih al-Manarzade's statements but, "omits them as a matter of good manners" (IV, 328).

The portion of Naima's history written after Hüseyin Köprülü's fall from the grand vezirate is incomplete. Here and there it contains Naima's working notes, and these serve to show something of his method.

For example, toward the end of the year 1068/began October 9, 1657, Naima had noted the following which was then carried into the printed editions:

From Naima VI, 361

Padishah of India

During this year Khurrem Shah (Jehan Shah) died. After a great and bloody struggle among his four princely sons for the sultanate of India, his younger son Evreng-zeyb [Aurangzeb], a man of wisdom and intelligence, became independent ruler through his own wise conduct and with the help of the officials. The "Accession of Shah Evreng-zeyb" and his "Adventures against his Brothers" are both extremely detailed [narratives]. They must be corrected and condensed and then inserted here. They are among those events that it is important to establish and copy out. This must not be neglected.

From this one would conclude that Naima possessed narratives of these two incidents, perhaps from Maanoğlu. But the next to the last sentence in the passage—"They are among those events that it is important to establish and copy out (the Turkish: *zabt ve tahriri mühimmattan olan vakayidendir*)."—is ambiguous. Without straining, the Turkish may also be read, "They are among those events that are to be established and copied out from the *mühimme* registers" (see Section 75). If this interpretation should prove to be acceptable, it means that for the later years, at any rate, Naima planned to use the *mühimme* registers as source material.

A comparable notation concerns the history of Vecihi, "The story of the vezir Fazlı Pasha must be located and inserted at this point. It is probably in Vecihi. This is not to be neglected" (VI, 383). Here we glimpse Naima at work at his desk.

When considering Naima or any other Ottoman historian who wrote before printing had been introduced into the empire, it is important to remember that history was not primarily written for the convenience of the individual reader as is the case with books written to be printed. Rather, history was primarily written to be read aloud. Listening to readings from history was a standard diversion in well-to-do Muslim society. It filled part of the function of the theater, the cinema, and television in the twentieth-century world.

Every important man—sultan, grand vezir, şeyhülislâm—in the Ottoman empire had his own *meclis,* his circle of friends, advisers, and supporters. History was read in such salons and, after an "event" had been read out, a general discussion might follow. Hüseyin Köprülü is said to have distinguished himself in such discussions (see Section 22). Even in the case of Naima, it is probably as much to such salon discussion as it is to the individual author-compiler that we should look to find the source of those opinions, good counsels, and words of equity that came to be incorporated into the various versions of the Ottoman "Chronicle of the Year 1000." When this circumstance is borne in mind, Naima's chronicle assumes new significance, for it may be held to embody segments of the *meclis* opinion of two of the most important families of the seventeenth-century Ottoman world, the Köprülü's *meclis* as transmitted by Naima and the Hocazade's [Hoca Efendi's] *meclis* as transmitted by Şarih al-Manarzade.

But this accretion of opinion, criticism, and illustrative anecdote is only an addition. The basic chronicle—the statement of events—in all versions of the chronicle proper goes back more or less to one type of source. It remains briefly to consider what was the basic source material of the bulk of Ottoman historiography after 1000 A.H.

75. **Ultimate Source**

As one's familiarity with Naima, the *Fezleke,* and other Ottoman historical writing of the seventeenth century increases, one more and more clearly perceives how often the underlying source for the account of an "event" is, in reality, an epitome [*telhis*] of an official document.[53] Such passages are distinct from those in which an official document is quoted verbatim, in part or in full.[54] These epitomes are made from reports and official correspondence reaching the sultan, or, perhaps more frequently, from orders and decrees issuing from the sultan or from the divan in the sultan's name.[55] Presumably a conscientious *vakayinüvis* would attempt to have access both to the *arz defteri* where correspondence addressed to the sultan was recorded and also to the *mühimme,* the proceedings of the imperial divan.

An example of a narrative based almost solely on official arz is the chronicle of the war in Crete as given in Naima and the *Fezleke.*

An example of a section whose underlying source is correspondence issuing from the sultan and the divan is the following:

In the year 1035/began October 3, 1625, both Naima (II, 401) and the *Fezleke* (II, 93), reproducing their common source, contain a short section, "Arrival of the English Ambassador." The *Fezleke* and Naima here are only two copies from one original. Nevertheless, enough variants have crept in to make accurate translation puzzling.

This brief passage is evidently a short entry from some official calendar or ledger—perhaps from the mühimme—which has been incorporated into the chronicle. It treats of one entire episode in Ottoman-English diplomacy. On the basis of the passage alone, it is to be translated as follows:

The Coming of the English Ambassador

The English king's ambassador came. In his letter he stated that he desired friendship and that he had succeeded his father as king. Since he had concluded a commercial pact with the Tunisians and Algerians, and since he also sought from the capital imperial permission for this, the kapıcıbaşı *was sent to the beylerbeyis of Algiers and Tunis.*

It was commanded also that in ports of the well-guarded dominions unjust charges should not be collected on demands contrary to the capitulations, for example under the name masdariye *and other pretexts, but that customs alone should be collected.*[56] *And it was commanded that since Husrev Pasha, who died as beylerbeyi of Algiers, had imprisoned the English who were in Algiers and at the Tunisian's side and had also taken several thousand* kuruş, *the aforementioned sum should be restored from the farmed revenues.*

And a letter was written and sent saying, "Ships of the English have taken twenty-four merchant ships en route from India to trade from the ports of the Yemen. Release those ships with the merchants aboard them and restore the ruined merchandise to its owners."

As is the case with entry after entry in Naima's version of the Ottomans' seventeenth-century chronicle, this laconic passage can be fully understood only when one had access to the original document or documents from which the entry was abstracted.

Here that original is a letter from Murad IV to Charles I, dated January, 1627.[57]

In translation, the letter reads as follows:

Pride of the great princes who follow Jesus,
Chosen one of the renowned grandees of the Messiah's community,
Arbiter of the affairs of the states of Christendom,
Trailer of the train's splendor and dignity,
Bearer of the marks of nobility and distinction,
King of England [Charles]—
may his last hours be ended with the Good![58]

With the arrival of the High Imperial Device may it be known that:

By the grace of the majestic Lord of the worlds and by the guidance of the honorable seal of the Prophets—upon whom the finest salute men can pronounce!—your letter of wonted good faith, which was sent to our high, felicitous threshold and our caliphate-pledged sublime porte which are the refuge of the sultans who hold the earth and the asylum of the hakans who possess the world, has now arrived by the hand of Sir Thomas Roe, the model of the princes of the Messiah's community, who is at present your ambassador at our capital.

Following old Ottoman law and enduring imperial customs, it has been translated and summarized by our great vezirs and illustrious ministers, submitted to our all-glorious, ever-felicitous presence, noted by our imperial notice, and epitomized by our gracious eye. Our noble intellect has comprehended from start to finish the events and topics written therein, and our benign understanding has stimulated the pleasing events written therein in whole and in detail.

Among what you say is: that, in addition to the mention and notice you take when recounting the condition of friendship long obtaining between our sublime porte and your fathers and grandfathers, you state that the government and kingship of those lands now, after your father, has devolved on you by inheritance and right, and that you for your part are even more steadfast in the way of your friendship and are staunch in the matter of peace and amity than was your father; that you strive daily further to reinforce the structure of peace and amity with our sublime porte, and that you have not left undone one atom of the deeds that call for the necessities of union and require the ceremonies of mutual understanding.

Our pure mind is pleased at this sort of friendly communication of yours, at your words of loyalty, and at the fact that in a happy hour you have come to rule your father's land. Also from our imperial side all manner of inclination [*and*] *favor towards you are clear and plain.*

You also state that your aforementioned ambassador who is now in our capital formerly made a treaty and an arrangement with the Tunisians and Algerians and drew up an agreement concerning the status of your merchants who come and go to and from those regions, and concerning their trade and the treatment which they are to be given—that a pledge was given by each side and that they [*thus*] *strengthened the peace* [*between us*].

Since this matter is most suitable and beneficial for both of the countries concerned, from our side assent to it has been shown and decision has been taken [*to ratify the treaty*].

You also desired that imperial orders be sent to the beylerbeyis of Tunis and Algiers to the effect that there shall be no infringement of this word and agreement so long as they are observed by the other party.

In consequence, our imperial commands containing all sorts of admonish-

ments have been sent to the two aforementioned beylerbeyis, and they have been strongly admonished not to transgress the compact given as above stated, not to infringe or evade the capitulations as your merchants buy and sell, coming or going as has been their custom.

Apart from this you state that certain governors and officials in the ports of our well-guarded dominions make various demands on your merchants contrary to the conditions and stipulations set down in the capitulations; that they demand money for a tax called masdariye *and for other pretexts. You state that when in accord with the imperial capitulations they [the English merchants] have paid their customs in the place where they have been accustomed to pay them, then they are again asked for money "for customs" at some other port also.*

WHEREFORE, since it is absolutely not our imperial will that in our propitious days and in the just order of our time anyone whosoever should presume to infringe the imperial capitulations, firm and severe imperial orders as requisite in this matter have been issued and instructions have been given and reaffirmed that there is to be no departure whatsoever from the terms of imperial capitulation as agreed between us; that to whatever place and whatever part of the well-guarded dominions English merchants shall come, every effort shall be made for them to discharge their affairs and proceed on in security and at ease, and that they [the Ottoman officials] shall be most careful that customs shall not be again demanded when the customs have once been paid and they have taken those unsold goods to another port, and not to make demands contrary to established usage.

You also communicate that the late Husrev Pasha, formerly beylerbeyi of Algiers, unjustly detained and imprisoned your consul at Algiers together with those of your men who were with him, and that he wrongly took from them several thousand kuruş *in violation of the Sacred Law and contrary to peace and amity.*

WHEREFORE, since it is plainer than day that our will is in no way [agreeable] to this sort of action and since at this moment there are at our capital a number of veteran soldiers, well-informed men, coming from Algiers, we have issued an imperial order that those men were to be questioned on this point. In fact, they have been brought in; each one of them has been given all manner of admonishment and reproof. When it had been confessed and defined by them, saying, "Let us pay the whole of the money that was taken, pay it from the farming money and the 1/5*th* *returns" and when they answered saying, "As soon as we get back let us set the consul and his men free," then in that tenor was our imperial order written, addressing the beylerbeyi of Algiers and embodying all sorts of reproof and punishment. He was admonished that he is not to neglect this matter and is speedily to set the consul free and to return the whole of the property that was taken; also that in the future he is not to pursue such conduct and acts but is to treat any consul whom you shall send to that region as was the former custom, and is to implement the rights of friendship as they ought to be implemented.*

And in short, as beseems our title Glory of Justice and pursuant to the capitulations, imperial orders have been written out and given to your aforementioned ambassador for the matters detailed in your newly arrived letter. Further, moreover, our imperial assent is not refused to propitious undertakings which conduce to friendship and benefit the merchants of both countries. It is certain that the necessary conditions of the mutual, longstanding peace between us will be observed as they should be.

However, there has come to our capital a report from our vezir Haydar Pasha, honored chief, famous commander, orderer of the world—May God exalted prolong his glory!—whom we have nominated and sent to defend the province of the Yemen, one of our far-reaching dominions. Also there has come a general complaint from the people of that province.

[Thus] it has been made known to the foot of our imperial throne, the abode of justice, that previously, in the time when the late Fazlı Pasha was the governor of the Yemen, ships belonging to subjects of your government, in violation of our imperial capitulation, attacked [Ottoman] merchants who were sailing from the region of India, fought them, took their ships, and caused damages of 600,000 kuruş. *They reported all this to the late vezir Fazlı Pasha. Since this affair was in violation of and contrary to Sacred and secular law and also to our imperial capitulations and since it necessitated the obtainment of an indemnity, the aforementioned [Fazlı Pasha] collected* 100,000 kuruş *from the masters of those ships, [recovering it] from that property which our merchants had lost. But* 500,000 kuruş *still remain as a debt to be discharged to our merchants.*

Up to the present time they [the English] have not repaid it. Instead, at present as if it were no concern of theirs, they have again outfitted ships, set out from your province [England], raided fourteen ships belonging to merchants of ours en route from the region of India to the ports of the

Yemen, enslaved the masters of those ships, and burned and destroyed their cargoes and provisions. At present there are seven armed ships—Flemish and ships of yours—at anchor in Mokha port, pretending to demand the return of the 100,000 kuruş *which Fazlı Pasha took.* [*So we have been informed*] *that they have dared and presumed to this sort of evil-doing and robbery, acts and behavior contrary to our imperial will.*

WHEREFORE, since it is by no means our imperial will that a single one of those ships belonging to merchants of our well-guarded dominions should be lost or that the goods and wares of a single one of those merchants should be destroyed, and since this was an unworthy action in violation of the conditions of peace obtaining between us and contrary to the conditions of friendship, there is written and set down this present our imperial letter so that you may—when all those merchants have been set free and the property and provisions that were taken have been entirely and wholly restored to their owners—thus fulfill the requirements of friendship and amity and conform to the rites of good faith and good will, strengthen the structure of the compact and the peace, and reinforce the foundation of the promise and of trust.

It is proper that when [*this letter arrives*] *and has been received, if it is your desire to remain steadfast in the way of fidelity, of securing friendship, of achieving the uttermost amity and agreement, and of furthering the union that you from early days until this moment have had with our firmly supported threshold and our strongly founded house, and if it is also your desire to give extraordinary attention and weight to the conditions of friendliness: then devote perfect attention and recognition, and extreme care of deed and word, to that aforementioned matter which has transpired contrary to our ever-propitious imperial will. Set free the fourteen ships of our merchants which, as aforesaid, were attacked and taken by the ships from England while en route from India to the port of Mokha in the Yemen, one of our well-guarded provinces, and also all of our merchants who were captured aboard those ships, with all their goods and supplies. Have the goods and wares of those merchants that were taken and have been lost or destroyed returned to their owners. Obey our imperial design nigh unto felicity, and conform to our ever fortunate, glory-pledge will. Let it be carefully considered that the result of such a course is that you will surely witness much of good and of benefit, propitious to your province and country and state.*

God willing, when this present letter of our imperial majesty, near unto felicity, shall reach you, you will send word to our capital by able and trustworthy men of yours, word of how you are heeding this matter and of how you will bestir yourself to return to their owners the whole of their goods and wares and to set free our merchants and their ships, of how you demonstrate your intentions towards our sublime capital, and of what good course and action you have taken in conforming to our imperial desire and our ever-propitious, fortune-near will.

This matter has also been communicated to your aforementioned ambassador. When he transmits it to you in detail, may its achievement be advanced and given importance by means in which you have complete confidence and which accord with the friendship of us two parties as well as with the establishment of peace and of the capitulation.

In the second decade of Cemaziyelevvel, *the year* 1036[59] *of the hegira of Muhammad upon whom be the finest benedictions and the most perfect praise.*

In the residence of Constantinople, the well-guarded.

On the basis of this document, the Naima passage translated above may now be understood in full.

The English ambassador "came," not from England, but officially to court for an audience.

In connection with the English treaty with Algiers and Tunis, the Ottomans sent an envoy to those "provinces" to convey imperial ratification of the treaty. Further Ottoman orders to Algiers and Tunis included abolition of extra-legal charges which were being demanded from the English. In Algiers the English consul and his men were to be released and restitution made to them.

In their turn, the Ottomans then present counter claims for English depredations on Ottoman shipping off the Yemen.

The purpose in presenting this document here is not to embark on the study of Ottoman-English relations in the seventeenth century, or even to provide a specimen of what the Turkish sources can offer to such a study; it is rather to illustrate the fact that, particularly after the year 1000 A.H., Ottoman historiography largely rests on a factual narrative constructed out of extracts from official documents. The prime requisite in studying that history, therefore, is not further editions of various versions of the chronicle to which one or another author's name may have become attached, perhaps somewhat adventitiously. The prime requisite is instead the edition of those documents themselves. They exist in surprising numbers. By far the most important series is the bound volumes of the proceedings of the Ottoman imperial divan.[60] It is much to be hoped that the entire series of these registers may eventually be issued in facsimile.

Until those registers are available, Naima, pieced out with other available versions of the Ottoman chronicle, will be of the greatest value to students. But it is only when the original documents are available that Naima himself will truly be able to speak.

NOTES

1. Naima, VI, appendix, p. 2. Note that this was written as late as 1703–4, when one would expect that the final draft of the earlier volume had long been completed.

2. Tahir Bey, *Osmanlı Müellifleri*, III, 152, states—evidently from first-hand knowledge—that the autograph of Naima's work up to 1066 A.H. was to be found in the Revan Köşkü of Topkapı Sarayı.

3. İbrahim Müteferrika categorically asserts in his publisher's preface that the *Tarih-i Naima* begins with 1000 A.H. The "Berlin Anonymous" in Wilhelm Pertsch, *Verzeichniss der Türkischen Handschriften der Königlichen Bibliothek zu Berlin*, p. 245, no. 216, an eye-witness account of the years 1099–1116/1687–1705, which is one of Hammer's principal sources for Hüseyin Köprülü and Rami Mehmed and also for the Edirne Incident, may just possibly be Naima's work.

4. "Transylvania Treaty" with Gabor, II, 133–4. The other treaty is also with Gabor, *ibid.*, 134–6. See *GOR*, IV, 464.

5. The Muslims of the Arab world are mentioned relatively seldom.

6. The sultan's departure on campaign, Naima I, 144; his return to Istanbul, *ibid.*, 176.

7. The sultan's departure on campaign, II, 187; his return to Istanbul, *ibid.*, 207. Compare Halil Edhem, "Sultan Osman Han Saninin Leh Seferine dair bir Kitabesi," *TOEM*, I (1329/1911), 223–32.

8. I, 245; II, 2 and *passim*. See also, A. Tveritinova, *Vosstanie Kara Yazızhı-Deli Khasana v Turcii*, and Mustafa Akdağ, *Celalî İsyanları 1550–1603*. These little-known Anatolian disorders did much to shape later Anatolian culture. See Pertev Naili, *Köroğlu Destanı*, especially pp. 101–3, 151–55.

9. See the study by J. H. Mordtmann, "Die jüdischen Kira im Serai der Sultane," *Mitteilungen des Seminars für Orientalische Sprachen*, XXXII (1929), 1–32.

10. *GOR*, VII, 328 *seq.*

11. See also *GOW*, 195 *seq.*

12. It furnishes amusing illustrations of the pitfalls of an oriental edition. For example, Naima ordinarily refers to Christians as "heathen," *kuffar*, the plural of *kafir*. In the *Fezleke*, *kuffar*, which has also a strong connotation in Turkish profanity, is replaced by the polite *âda*, "enemies." That the change from *kuffar* to *âda* was made by the overly squeamish nineteenth-century editor of the *Fezleke* is shown by a passage in *Fezleke* II, 314 (Naima, IV, 252), where the statement in the former, "among the enemy of the sea" (*âda-i bahrda*) is senseless until one realizes that in the correct statement "on the sea-shore" (kenar-i bahrda), the word *kenar*, meaning shore, has been misread as *kuffar* and then edited to *âda*.

13. It includes:

Naima		cf. *Fezleke,*
	I, 99	I, 34
,,	I, 102	,, I, 41
,,	I, 385	,, I, 227
,,	I, 430	,, I, 267
,,	II, 99	,, I, 347
,,	IV, 231	,, II, 295
,,	IV, 239	,, II, 305–6

14. Compare the manuscript listed (from Manisa) in K. Süssheim, "Aus anatolischen Bibliotheken," *Beiträge zur Kentniss des Orients,* VII (1909), 83.

15. Hence, such statements as that of Halil Edhem, *TOEM,* I (1911), 228, that Naima's account of Osman II's Polish campaign (see Section 65) is "based on" the *Fezleke* require revision.

16. Tayyarzade, *Tarih,* III, 325.

17. Hasanbeyzade is said to have died in 1046/began June 5, 1636; *GOW,* 174.

18. Peçevî's chronicle is now available in new letters, *Peçevî Tarihi,* Murat Uraz, ed.

19. *GOW,* 190–1.

20. Naima, IV, 10.

21. Naima, II, 296–7.

22. Peçevî had left Istanbul the previous year to return to his homeland (Hungary). His term of office in Bosnia has not previously been known; see F. Kraelitz, "Der osmanische Historiker Ibrahim Pecevi," *Islam,* VIII (1918), 252–60.

23. GOW, 190, adds the month, Saban (May 24–June 21, 1657).

24. The family tree:

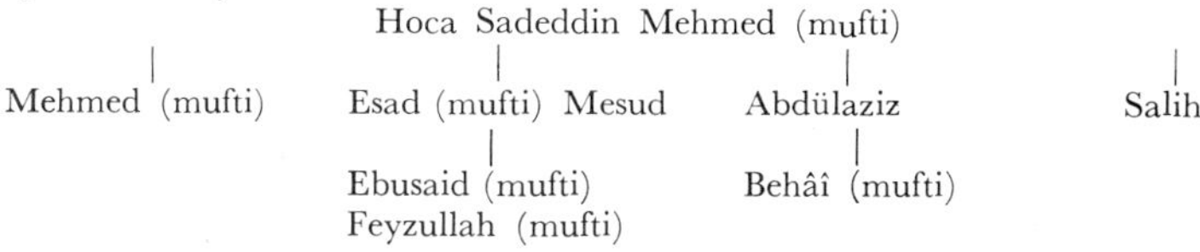

25. Şarih al-Manarzade in Naima, IV, 82 *seq.*

26. Şarih al-Manarzade in Naima, IV, 7.

27. *GOR,* V, 342–5.

28. Şarih al-Manarzade in Naima, IV, 85–6.

29. Şarih al-Manarzade in Naima, IV, 451.

30. Şarih al-Manarzade in Naima, V, 230–1.

31. Naima, VI, 22.

32. *GOW,* 190.

33. *İstanbul Kataloglarι,* pp. 119–20.

34. For example, Naima, VI, 12, where Ebusaid's inability to pronounce the sound of "r" is illustrated. Another example is in Naima, II, 183.

35. Şarih al-Manarzade in Naima—clearcut instances are, Naima II, 82, 129, 348, 402, 408; Naima, III, 186, 209, 229, 256, 287, 294, 317, 336, 338, 358, 363, 368, 399, 423, 460; Naima, IV, 12, 36, 41, 63, 83, 179, 203, 278, 285, 288, 290, 294, 304, 307, 313, 327, 330, 332, 333, 335, 358, 388, 419, 432, 437, 451, 458; Naima, V, 24, 31, 35, 43, 45, 62, 69, 73, 107, 130, 132, 138, 142, 148, 168, 174, 189, 212, 216, 223, 231, 240, 246, 277, 282, 294, 323, 326, 353, 375, 409, 428; Naima, VI, 4, 31.

36. *GOW,* 227–8. He is cited in Naima, IV, 311; VI, 168, 176, 183, 221, 258 and 266.

37. *GOW,* 209–10; cited in Naima, VI, 185, 215 and 304.

38. *GOW,* 278; cited in Naima, VI, 304, 324 and 362.

39. *GOW,* 174.

40. Hasanbeyzade is cited directly in Naima, I, 214, 227, 243, 247, 309, 376, 387, 388; Naima, II, 25, 163, 167, 205, 252, 293. Certain of these passages, for example, Naima, I, 247 and 309, are confusing because they are left in the first person where "I" is Hasanbeyzade and not Naima.

41. *GOW,* 204; cited in Naima, I, 247; Naima, IV, 372, 402; Naima, VI, 134, 149, 157, 159, 185, 191, 202, 226, 243, 293, 304, 307, 422.

42. Assuming that he was about seventy at his death.

43. Naima, III, 148–9, 176–80.

44. Naima, III, 179; all subsequent page references from Naima throughout this section will be given in text.

45. Naima, VI, appendix, p. 22, where it is evident that Salih Agha and Naima were personal foes. On Salih Agha, a Damascene Arab who had been one of Maanoğlu's personal staff, see *SO*, III, 204.

46. See Section 21; important sections in which Naima cites Maanoğlu are Naima, II, 93–4, 119–23, 148; Naima, III, 148, 179–80, 242, 385–92; Naima, IV, 293–4; Naima, V, 102–6, 249–55, 342–7, 448; Naima, VI, 125–7, 147, 168, 185, 208, 237, 410–11.

47. See the story of the confiscation of a wealthy Egyptian's estate two years before Maanoğlu went forth from the Palace; Naima, V, 448–52.

48. Naima, VI, 125–7. For an example of Cevrî's chronograms, see Naima, V, 266.

49. See *ODT*, I, 551.

50. Naima, VI, 224, reproduced in *SO*, IV, 169.

51. Naima, VI, 242, reproduced in *SO*, IV, 168.

52. Naima, IV, 63.

53. Consult J. H. Mordtmann, *Ungarische Jahrbücher*, VIII (1928), 164 (review of *GOW*).

54. For example, in Naima, I, 455–58. Compare with L. Fekete, *Türkische Schriften aus dem Archive des Palatins Nikolaus Esterhazy*, pp. 3, 207; Naima, II, 137–40, and with Fekete, *Esterhazy*, pp. 7, 213.

55. For example, Raşid, *Tarih*, III, 239, dates the death of Rami Mehmed (at Rhodes) by the order for the confiscation of his estate as it was written at Istanbul.

56. See *ODT*, II, 413.

57. A copy of the original (Oxford, Ethé no. 2288/Bodl. Ms. Turc. a l'(R) no. 8) was kindly made available by Professor Paul Wittek. A portion of the text has been edited, presumably from a file copy, in Ahmed Feridun Bey, *Mecmua-i münşeat-i selatin*, 2nd ed. (Istanbul, 1275/1858–9), II, 471–2.

58. That is, may he become a Muslim before he dies.

59. January 30–February 8, 1627.

60. On these *mühimme* registers, see Midhat Sertoglu, *Muhteva bakimindan Başvekalet Arşivi*, pp. 15–22; and the important article by Uriel Heyd summarized in *Akten des XXIV. Internationalen Orientalisten-Kongresses München 1957*, Herbert Franke ed. (Wiesbaden, 1959), pp. 389–91, "The Mühimme Defteri (Register of Degrees): A Major Source for the Study of Ottoman Administration."

Conclusion

In the Ottoman world of the late seventeenth and early eighteenth centuries Mustafa Naima Efendi ranked as a man of ability and attainments. His reputation today rests solely upon the history that he compiled. It is improper to overpraise him for all of the work's good points since many of them, including some of the points for which Naima is most praised today, came not from his pen, but from those of his several predecessors, identified and anonymous. Conversely, it is improper to criticize Naima alone for the many imperfections in his work, since many of these, too, are due to his predecessors. He took what was bequeathed to him, material and form. He improved upon both, increasing and evaluating the material, rationalizing and simplifying form.

Naima lived at a time when the Ottoman state was internally weak. His work recognizes that fact and is addressed to it. In grand design and in detail the *Tarih-i Naima* was intended to help improve matters, to strengthen the state. That its effect on the course of the Ottoman state was probably almost nil is beside the point; it was a patriotic attempt to serve faith and state and not simply an ambitious individual's production.

Every concrete suggestion that Naima offers is taken from the arsenal of Muslim-Ottoman civilization.[1] Unlike İbrahim Müteferrika, who had been a Hungarian, Naima has not seen contemporary Europe with his own eyes and does not realize how rapidly the Ottomans are being outpaced. Unlike Kâtip Çelebi, who was a genius, Naima cannot intellectually comprehend what a threat European power and technique constitute.

Hence Naima may fairly be called parochial in the sense that his horizon in time and space was limited to his own world, the lands of Islam. But this is scarcely a criticism. There have been few able men throughout history, and today, when advances in transportation and communication have annihilated distance, there still are few men of whom the same statement would not be true, whatever the world in which they live.

From one point of view, Naima gives little evidence that he was in direct personal contact with the best that Islamic literature might have offered him—his knowledge of Ibn Khaldûn excepted. And this, too, is readily understandable. Naima was a practical man. His education and his times led him to the later Muslim compilers; again he was not a genius, as Kâtip Çelebi had been, and did not attempt to master the whole of the classics of Islam. But from another point of view, regarding Naima only within the frame of his own time and place, it appears that he did exemplify what the modern mind tends to accept as the "best" of that vanished Ottoman world. He was liberal, rational, and constructive, and he held his views at a time when the good things of life were all too likely to end up in the hands of those who were reactionary, doctrinaire, and fanatic.

These circumstances, beyond all others, make Naima the almost perfect analogue for many equally patriotic but less articulate Ottoman figures of the eighteenth and nineteenth centuries. Loyal, liberal Muslim Ottomans, possessed of courage that no defeats and disappointments seemingly could destroy, but oblivious of, and unable to grasp, the new *capacity* for devilment that the Franks had achieved, they persisted in trying to build with the old tools until new tools were forcibly thrust into their reluctant, unaccustomed hands.

NOTE

1. And not from Turkish culture. Like all upper-class Ottomans, Naima did not consider himself a "Türk," but rather an Ottoman. See for example, Naima, III, 11, 204, 236, 298, 335 and 337. Compare with Section 62.

Bibliography

Abou-El-Haj, Rifa'at A. "Ottoman Diplomacy at Karlowitz," *Journal of the American Oriental Society*, 87/4 (December, 1967), 498–512.

———"The Reisülkuttab and Ottoman Diplomacy at Karlowitz," Ph.D. dissertation, Princeton University, 1963.

Adıvar, Abdulhak Adnan. *Osmanlı Türklerinde İlim.* 2nd printing. Istanbul, 1943.

———*Tarih Boyunca İlim ve Din.* 2 vols. Istanbul, 1944.

Akdağ, Mustafa. *Celalî İsyanları 1550–1603.* Ankara, 1963.

Aksüt, Ali Kemali. See Koçi Bey.

Aktepe, M. Münir. "Naimâ Tarihi'nin yazma nushaları hakkında," *Tarih Dergisi*, I/1 (1949), 35–52.

Arberry, A. J. *The History of Sufism.* London, 1942.

Asım, Necip. "Osmanlı Tarih-nüvislerı ve Müverrihleri," *Tarih-i Osmani Encümen Mecmuası*, II (1329/1911), 425–35, 498–9.

Babinger, Franz. "Shejeh Bedr ed-din, der Sohn des Richters von Simaw," *Der Islam*, XI (1921), 1–106.

———"Ein türkischer Stiftungsbrief des Nerkesi vom Jahre 1029/1620," *Mitteilungen zur Osmanischen Geschichte*, I/2–3 (1921–2), 151–66.

———*Die Geschichtsschreiber der Osmanen und Ihre Werke.* Leipzig, 1927.

Banarlı, Nihad Sami. See Gönensay, Hıfzı Tevfik.

Belin, M. "Bibliographie Ottomane," *Journal Asiatique*, 6. Ser. XI (June, 1868), 465–91.

Berker, Aziz. See Penah Efendi.

Birge, J. K. *The Bektashi Order of Dervishes.* Hartford, 1937.

Björkman, W. *Beiträge zur Geschichte der Staatskanzlei im islamischen Ägypten.* Hamburg, 1928.

Bodman, Herbert. *Political Factions in Aleppo 1760–1826.* Chapel Hill, 1963.

Canib, Ali. *Naima Tarihi.* Istanbul, 1927.

Carali, Paolo. *Fakhr al-Din II Principe del Libano e la Corte di Toscana, 1605–1635.* 2 vols. Rome, 1936–8.

Cevdet, Ahmed. *Osmanlı Tarih ve Müverrihleri.* Istanbul, 1314/1896–7.

Demombynes, M. G. *La Syrie á l'epoque des mamelouks.* Paris, 1923.

Deny, J. *Sommaire des Archives Turques du Caire.* Cairo, 1930.

Duda, H. "Na'īmā," *Türkische Post*, III (1928), No. 324.

Edhem, Halil. "Sultan Osman Han Saninin Leh Seferine dair bir Kitabesi," *Tarih-i Osmani Encümeni Mecmuası*, I (1329/1911), 223–32.

Edip, Halide. *Memoirs.* New York, no date.

Encyclopaedia of Islam. 4 vols. Leiden-London, 1913–36. *Supplement*, Leiden, 1938.

———New Edition. Leiden, 1960–

Evliya Çelebi. *Seyahatname.* 10 vols. Istanbul, 1314/1896–1938.

Fekete, L. *Türkische Schriften aus dem Archive des Palatins Nikolaus Esterhàzy.* Budapest, 1933.

Feridun Bey, Ahmed. *Mecmua-i münşeat-i selatin.* 2nd. ed. 2 vols. Istanbul, 1275/1858–9.

Forrer, Ludwig. "Handschriften osmanischer Historiker in Istanbul," *Der Islam* XXVI (1940–42), 173–220.

Fraser, Charles. See Naima, Mustafa.
Gerçek, Selim Nüzhet. *Türk Matbaacılığı*. Istanbul, 1939.
Gibb, E. J. W. *A History of Ottoman Poetry*. 6 vols. London, 1900–09.
Gönensay, Hıfzı Tevfik and Nihad Sami Banarlı. *Türk Edebiyatı Tarihi (Başlangıçtan Tanzimata Kadar)*. Istanbul, 1944.
Grunebaum, G. von. *Medieval Islam*. Chicago, 1946.
Grzegorzewski, J. Z. *Sidzyallatòw Rumelijskich Epoki Wyprawy Wiedenskiej, akta tureckie*. Lwow, 1912.
Hammer, J. von. *Des Osmanischen Reiches Staatsverfassung und Staatsverwaltung*. 2 vols. Vienna, 1815.
———*Geschichte des Osmanischen Reiches*. 10 vols. Pesth, 1827–35.
Heyd, Uriel. "The Mühimme Defteri (Register of Degrees): A Major Source for the Study of Ottoman Administration," *Akten des XXIV. Internationalen Orientalisten-Kongresses München 1957*, Herbert Franke, ed. Wiesbaden, 1959.
Hitti, Philip K. *History of the Arabs*. 2nd ed. London, 1940.
Ibn Khaldûn. *The Muqaddimah*, Franz Rosenthal, trans. 3 vols. Princeton, 1958.
İslam Ansiklopedisi. Istanbul, 1941–.
İsmail Pasha. *İzah al-meknum*, Şerefeddin Yaltkaya and Kilisli Rifat Bilge, eds. Istanbul, 1945.
Itzkowitz, Norman. "Mehmed Raghib Pasha: The Making of an Ottoman Grand Vezir," unpublished Ph.D. dissertation, Princeton University, 1959.
———"Eighteenth-Century Ottoman Realities," *Studia Islamica*, XVI (1962), 73–94.
Karal, Enver Ziya. *Selim III. ıün Hatt-ı Humayunlaıı*. Ankara, 1942.
Karslızade, Cemaleddin. *Ayine-i zurefa*. Istanbul, 1314/1896–7.
Kâtip Çelebi. *Düstûrü'l-'amel*. Istanbul, 1280/1863.
———"Hâgî Chalfa's Dustûru'l-amel," W. F. A. Behrnauer, trans. *Zeitschrift der Deutschen morgenlandischen Gesellschaft*, XI (1857), 111–32.
———*Fezleke-i Tarih*. 2 vols. Istanbul, 1286–7/1869–70.
———*The Balance of Truth*, G. L. Lewis, trans. London, 1957.
Kemankeş Kara Mustafa Pasha. "Kemankeş Kara Mustafa Pasa Lahiyası," Faik Reşat Unat, ed. *Türk Tarih Vesikaları*, I/6 (1942), 433–80.
Kınalızade, Âli Efendi. *Ahlak-ı alâî*. 3 vols. Bulaq, 1248/1832–3.
Koçi Bey. *Koçi Bey Risalesi*, Ali Kemali Aksüt, ed. Istanbul, 1939.
Köprülü, M. Fuad. "Bizans Müesseselerinin Osmanlı Müesseselerine Tesiri Hakkında Bazı Mülahazalar," *Türk Hukuk ve Iktisat Tarihi Mecmuası*, I (1931), 165–313.
———(Köprülüzade, Mehmed Fuad). *Divan Edebiyat. Antolojisi*. Istanbul, 1934.
———(Köprülü, F.). "Anadolu Selçukluları tarihinin yerli kaynakları," Belleten, VII/27 (1943), 379–522.
Koran. J. M. Rodwell, trans. London, 1933.
Kraelitz, F. "Der osmanische Historiker Ibrahim Pecevi," *Der Islam*, VIII (1918), 252–60.
Kurat, Akdes Nimet. *Prut Seferi ve Barışı*. 2 vols. Ankara, 1951–3.
Lewis, G. L. "The Utility of Ottoman Fethnames," *Historians of the Middle East*, Bernard Lewis and P. M. Holt, eds. London, 1962, pp. 192–6.
———See Kâtip Çelebi.
Lybyer, Albert H. *The Government of the Ottoman Empire in the Time of Suleyman the Magnificent*. Cambridge, Mass., 1913.
MacCullum, F. Lyman. See Süleyman Çelebi.
Mardin, Ebülula. *Ahmet Cevdet Paşa*. Istanbul, 1946.
Meninski, F. *Lexicon arabico-persico-turcicum*, B. Jenisch, ed. 4 vols. Vienna, 1780–1802.
Miller, Barnette. *The Palace School of Muhammad the Conqueror*. Cambridge, Mass., 1941.
Mordtmann, J. H. "Miszellen," *Der Islam*, XII (1922), 222–5.
———*Ungarische Jahrbücher*, VIII (1928), 164–7. (Review).
———"Die jüdischen Kira im Serai der Sultane," *Mitteilungen des Seminars für Orientalische Sprachen* (Berlin), XXXII (1929), 1–32.
Mustafa Nuri Pasha. *Netayic el-vukuat*. 4 vols. Istanbul, 1327/1909.
Naili, Pertev. *Köroğlu Destanı*. Istanbul, 1931.

Naima, Mustafa. *Tarih-i Naima*. Müteferrika Press, 2 vols. Constantinople, 1147/1733; 2nd ed. Amire Press, 6 vols. Constantinople, 1280/1863–4; 3rd ed. Amire Press, 6 vols. Constantinople, 1281–3/1864–6. New Letters (*Naima Tarihi*), Zuhuri Danışman, ed. 6 vols. Istanbul, 1967–9.
———*Annals of the Turkish Empire from 1591–1659 of the Christian Era*, Charles Fraser, trans. London, 1832.
Ohsson, M. D'. *Tableau général de l'Empire ottoman*. 7 vols. Paris, 1788–1824.
Olmstead, A. T. *Jesus in the Light of History*. New York, 1942.
Oppenheim, Max von. *Die Beduinen*. 4 vols. in 5. Berlin-Leipzig, 1939–68.
Pakalın, Mehmet Zeki. *Osmanlı Tarih Deyimleri ve Terimleri Sözlüğü*. 3 vols. Istanbul, 1946 .
Peçevî, İbrahim. *Peçevî Tarihi*, Murat Uraz, ed. 2 vols. Istanbul, 1968–9.
Penah Efendi. "Mora Ithilâli Tarihçesi," Aziz Berker, ed. *Türk Tarih Vesikaları*, II (1942–3), 63–80, 153–60, 228–40, 309–20, 385–400, 437–80.
Pertsch, Wilhelm. *Verzeichniss der Türkischen Handschriften der Königlichen Bibliothek zu Berlin*. Berlin, 1889.
Raşid, Mehmed. *Tarih-i Raşid*. 2nd ed. 6 vols. Istanbul, 1282/1865.
Redhouse, James W. *A Turkish and English Lexicon*. Constantinople, 1921.
Refik, Ahmed. *Alimler ve Sanatkârlar*. Istanbul, 1924.
———*Hicri On İkinci Asırda Istanbul Hayatı*. Istanbul, 1930.
———*Hicri On Altıncı Asırda Istanbul Hayatı*. Istanbul, 1935.
Rodwell, J. M. See *Koran*.
Rosenthal, Franz. See Ibn Khaldûn.
Rypka, J. *Baqí als Ghazeldichter*. Prague, 1926.
Salim Efendi. *Tezkere-i Salim*. Istanbul, 1314/1896–7.
Sami, Şemseddin. *Kamus el-Âlem*. 6 vols. Constantinople, 1306–16/1889–98.
Selânikî, Mustafa Efendi. *Tarih-i Selânikî*. Istanbul, 1281/1863.
Sertoğlu, Midhat. *Muhteva bakımından Başvekalet Arşivi*. Ankara, 1955.
Storey, C. A. *Persian Literature*. 2 vols. in 3. London, 1927–58.
Süleyman Çelebi. *Mevlid-i şerif*, F. Lyman MacCullum, trans. Istanbul, 1950.
Sürreya, Mehmed. *Sicill-i Osmanî*. 4 vols. Constantinople. 1308–15/1890–98.
Süssheim, K. "Aus anatolischen Bibliotheken," *Beiträge zur Kentniss des Orients*, VII (1909), 77–88.
Tahır, Bursalı Mehmed. *Osmanlı Müellifleri*. 3 vols. Istanbul, 1334–8/1915–19.
Tayyarzade, Ahmed Atâ. *Tarih-i Atâ*. 5 vols. Istanbul, 1291–3/1874–6.
Türkiye Cumhuriyeti. Maarif Vekilliği Kütüphaneler Müdürlüğü Tasnif Komisyonu *İstanbul Kütüphaneleri Tarih-Cografya Yazmaları Katalogları*. Istanbul, 1943–
———Kültür Bakanlığı Topkapı Sarayı Müzesi. *Arşiv Kılavuzu*. 2 fasc. Istanbul, 1938–40.
Tvertinova, A. *Vosstanie Kara Yazızhı-Deli Khasana v Turcii*. Moscow, 1946.
Uluçay, M. Çagatay. *Saruhan'd Eşkiyalik ve Halk Hareketleri XVII. Asırda*. Istanbul, 1944.
Unat, Faik Reşat. See Kemankeş Kara Mustafa Pasha.
Uzunçarşılı, İ. H. *Osmanlı Devleti Teşkilâtından Kapukulu Ocakları*. 2 vols. Ankara, 1943–4.
———*Osmanlı Devletinin Saray Teşkilâtı*. Ankara, 1945.
———*Osmanlı Devletinin Merkez ve Bahriye Teşkilâtı*. Ankara, 1948.
Wittek, Paul. *Mitteilungen zur Osmanischen Geschichte*, 1/4 (1922), 240–44. (Review)
———*Der Islam*, XX (1932), 197–207. (Review)
———*Das Fürstentum Mentesche*. Istanbul, 1934.
———*The Rise of the Ottoman Empire*. London, 1938.
Wright, Walter. *Ottoman Statecraft*. Princeton, 1935.
Zinkeisen, Johann Wilhelm. *Geschichte des Osmanischen Reiches in Europa*. 7 vols. Gotha, 1840–63